PREDICTABLE INCOME

PREDICTABLE INCOME

A Practical System For Building Multiple Income Streams So You're Never Dependent On One Job

Aaron Ross, Matt A. Smith,
and Camila Farani

JONES MEDIA PUBLISHING

Free Reader Gift

Why do some people turn their skills into consulting income... while others stay stuck doing the same work for the same pay?

It's not because they're smarter. It's not because they work harder.
And it's definitely not because they got lucky. The difference is in how they package what they already know.

Most people never see this...So they keep doing more work, hoping income follows.

It doesn't. Meanwhile, others take the exact same skills...
And turn them into high-value consulting offers.

If you've ever thought, "I know I'm capable of more... I just don't see the path..."

This will help. You'll see real, simple examples of how people are doing it right now.

Download the free guide here:
PredictableIncome.io/consulting

CHAPTER 1: REBOOT

"Plans are nothing; planning is everything."

— Dwight D. Eisenhower

Venice Beach. Gray skies. Cold air. Matt sat in a conference room with his team, planning their biggest growth year yet. He had been there from the beginning as the third employee, a key builder who helped turn a rough idea into a fast-growing business. A decade in, it felt like family. The past two years were a blur as sales and workload exploded. The pace was relentless. When the company sold for $70M, it looked like a win. Matt thought it would change his life, but it didn't. His payout was small, the celebration short. Twelve months after the sale, things slowed down. The new owners wanted results fast. On the last afternoon of the off-site, one of the senior leaders pulled Matt aside and told him they wanted a change. They blamed him for the slowdown. The same person who had built the core of the business was now the one taking the fall.

The conversation hurt. Years of loyalty, late nights, and sacrifice were gone in minutes. They offered Matt a minor role, just a paycheck, no leadership. He accepted. Pride doesn't pay the rent.

Six months later, the next call came: "Goodbye. Thank you for your service." And with that, it was over. His calendar emptied, messages stopped, and the familiar rhythm of work disappeared. But he wasn't starting from zero. After the initial shock, Matt turned to the consulting practice he had built on the side. Within three months, he signed a new freelance contract, worth $100,000 a year.

He had been fired, but he refused to be broken. The years of preparation had paid off. He didn't have to beg for another job. When the company cut ties, his own work caught him. The services business he built became a dependable source of income tied only to his abilities, not to a company's budget.

Work has changed. Income strategy has not. Jobs are no longer guaranteed, nor are they tied to multi-year contracts. They are short-term arrangements that can end at any time. That doesn't make companies evil. It makes them rational. They optimize for speed, cost, and output. When conditions change, roles disappear.

The risk is not AI or outsourcing. The risk is building your entire life around one paycheck.

Predictable Income is the playbook for removing that risk.

The authors have experienced the highs and lows of employment, entrepreneurship, and investing. We have launched startups that never made it past the early days. We have had years with more income than we expected and years with none. Through it all, one truth surfaced: there had to be an option between clinging to one employer and risking everything to become a full-time founder.

For many of us, the options seem limited: stay in corporate life or leap into entrepreneurship. The answer lies somewhere in between. Keep the stability of a job. Add a controllable freelance line. This combination gives you a stronger position than either extreme.

This book provides a modern, formal framework for building multiple income streams. There's endless chatter about "multiple income sources," yet scarce guidance on how to create them. Gurus stay vague to protect themselves by avoiding specifics. If they never speak in detail, they can never be wrong.

Predictable Income rejects that. We explain which sources to build, which accounts to open, and the numbers that lead to *Predictable Income.*

The Income Operating System

Predictable Income is both the framework and the outcome we will achieve together. *Income Operating System* is the practical framework built around three income sources:

- Employment provides structure and steady cash flow.
- Freelancing offers fast, flexible income tied to your expertise.
- Investing turns income into assets, assets into returns, and returns into liquid wealth.

You establish one cash flow stream, plant seeds in the others, and sequence your way to a dependable income base.

What Is an Operator?

Operator: A professional who treats income like a business and builds earning power with intent, instead of relying on one employer for stability. Operators build multiple income streams while pursuing quantifiable earnings and portfolio targets.

Operators thrive on structure, seeking defined mission outcomes, detailed plans, and repeatable systems. They train daily, expect volatility, and stay ready for hard evolutions. They sharpen skills, build optionality, and keep operating when conditions tighten.

If you want a stable, high-earning career in today's economy, you need to think and act like an Operator.

How to Use This Book

Think of this book as your pilot's checklist. Read in sequence. Capture ideas. Pause mid-chapter when something clicks, and apply it immediately. Pair audio and print versions to reinforce the learning. Review your income streams regularly to see what's working, what's stalling, and where to adjust.

The full audiobook is available here:

PredictableIncome.io/audio

Use code "income" at checkout to receive it at no cost.

The Road Ahead

What comes next is the plan to move your income forward. This book will teach you how to run your annual income missions and stack them year after year. These missions form your income infrastructure, a foundation that strengthens with experience. You'll secure better roles, complete high-value freelance work, and build an investment portfolio designed for sustainable growth. The goal is to achieve consistent six-figure earnings and build a seven-figure investment portfolio to weather any disruption.

Turn the page. Let's get to work.

CHAPTER 2: THE SYSTEM

"Systems run the world. Goals may give you direction, but systems are what create progress."

— James Clear

It started with exhaustion. Aaron sat in a large rented home in Los Angeles, staring at another month of uneven invoices and late payments, wondering how he ended up here. Years of freelancing, consulting, coaching, workshops, and books felt productive. But none of it truly moved him forward. Each income stream operated in isolation. Some paid well, others barely covered rent, and none were connected.

One night, he opened a blank spreadsheet and listed every way he made money. Seven columns. One messy map. He drew lines between them, tracing how each activity fed into the others, where energy leaked, and where exponential growth might be hiding in plain sight. Then it clicked. Books spread the ideas, creating demand. Demand led to speaking engagements, consulting work, and ultimately revenue. Writing remained central, keeping the entire chain connected and moving.

Rather than chasing new projects, he focused on optimizing the ones that supported each other. Cash flow stabilized, and opportunities became repeatable. For the first time, his income supported itself without constant scrambling. He realized wealth was not about adding more, but about linking what already worked.

The Income Flywheel

It moves in a loop: Earn, Learn, Invest. Every time you complete the whole loop, your financial momentum grows.

Earn represents your job. A consistent paycheck provides stability and creates financial runway.

Learn represents freelancing. Side income becomes an opportunity for skill building, refining your entrepreneurial toolkit.

Invest to complete the loop. Consistent income and deliberate investing turn effort into a self-reinforcing cycle.

There have never been more ways to earn, and that is the problem. An excess of choices can obscure the path forward. Without structure, your attention scatters across disconnected initiatives.

Having a system brings focus. It helps you channel energy into moves that actually increase income.

Predictable Income is built around three central streams. Your objective is to build each one up to generate $100,000 in annual income.

Every plan has a starting point, and it's you. You're the constant across all the ways you earn. Each income source should match your strengths, interests, and relationships.

Your job, freelance work, and investments should function as parts of one coordinated plan. If you work in tech sales, your freelancing could involve CRM consulting or helping startups develop effective sales processes. Your investment capital might tilt toward technology businesses. Each piece builds on the last. You'll advance faster, earn more, and waste less time.

This alignment transforms income generation into a focused, targeted effort. When your skills, income, and assets all point in the same direction, growth speeds up. You are not starting over each time. You are gaining more power over how you earn.

The job is your anchor. It pays predictably and comes with perks. But it can be restrictive due to contracts and time commitments. Relying on it alone caps your growth. Freelancing offers flexibility and can be lucrative, but it's unforgiving without structure. Investing scales results without scaling hours, but it demands significant capital and time before results become meaningful.

Each fills the gaps of the others, creating balance and resilience that lasts.

Income Order of Operations

Pursuing all three income sources simultaneously can quickly lead to burnout. The key is sequencing. Focus intensely on one stream at a time.

Start with employment to secure benefits and a reliable paycheck. Develop expertise that creates value and negotiate for it.

your consulting career, you will work with hundreds of clients. The regular flow of projects becomes a meaningful share of your lifetime earnings. The final $2M comes from ownership inside your investing stream: small business acquisitions that throw off meaningful income.

Annual missions focus execution within set timeframes. You don't need to earn $10M next year. Do the work across the three streams. Over time, the $10M in earnings leads to a $2.5M portfolio.

The target matters because it enforces discipline, not because it's a finish line. It gives you a clear benchmark to judge whether each role change, freelance cycle, or ownership decision moves you forward or sets you back. Once the math is visible, decisions sharpen. The work evolves from guessing to execution.

Becoming a millionaire may seem like the ultimate goal, but in today's world, that number doesn't hold the same significance it once did. A million in cash, investments, or net worth no longer guarantees stability. The goal isn't a number. It's durable wealth built from income, assets, and habits that keep paying you for life.

Decades ago, a million could buy economic security. Today, it's just a milestone, a checkpoint on the path to true financial independence.

Instead of optimizing for status, focus on execution and business building. Build multiple income engines, focus your expertise, and allocate capital into assets that produce returns across market cycles. This approach builds confidence and flexibility, helping you navigate financial challenges.

Rule 1: Keep your day job. It funds everything else.

Rule 2: Grow your side income with repeatable, consistent progress. Test, adapt, and expand your operation over time.

Rule 3: Invest in liquid assets aggressively. Income is fickle; stable liquid assets are not.

The State of American Finances

Most Americans talk about financial success in abstract terms, but few can define it in numbers. In the United States, the median household income is approximately $74,500. To reach the top 1% of earners, a household needs around $650,000.[1]

Only 58% of Americans own any stock, and among those who do, the median portfolio is roughly $40,000.[2] Meanwhile, the national saving rate hovers near 4%[3]—far below the recommended 15% to 20% for long-term financial health.[4]

Without meaningful income growth and consistent investing, major goals like homeownership, career flexibility, or retirement remain out of reach.

Before you can outperform the average, you need to understand where the average actually sits. Real economic security begins once you move past these baselines.

Income First and Foremost

Early in your career, income matters more than net worth. Wealth only grows after you've built the ability to earn consistently. When income stops, everything else fails. Savings shrink, bills accumulate, and stability disappears faster than most people expect.

Focus on building earning power before pursuing investments. The objective is reliable income that can adjust to role changes, market shifts, and different stages of life. Until that base exists, every other financial strategy is fragile.

Once income is consistent, asset accumulation follows. You move from dependence on a single paycheck to systems that generate cash across multiple streams. Know how to earn. Maintain that capability. It is the foundation on which everything else rests.

Operator Online

Those who are broke remain broke by repeating the same poor decisions year after year. They overspend, save too little, and depend on jobs that could vanish overnight. Then they act shocked when life punches them in the mouth. An Operator sees what's coming and prepares.

As an Operator, you take ownership of your work, capabilities, and income. You don't wait for a boss to fix your life. You don't blame the market or the economy. You make a plan, and you stick to it.

When you live this way, income becomes far more predictable. You know where every dollar goes, which skills pay the most, and which opportunities are worth pursuing.

So many of us move through periods where the days blur together and we find ourselves waiting for something to change.

You form habits that pay dividends. You nurture relationships that open doors. You develop income streams that remain stable even when your job situation changes.

That's the Operator path.

It isn't easy. When conditions turn, and they always do, you're prepared.

CHAPTER 3: EMPLOYMENT OS

"Income is the outcome of value,
not the reward for time."

— Naval Ravikant

Matt was in line to board a flight at LAX when an email from his CEO client came through. The contract was terminated, effective immediately. It was three days before Christmas.

Months earlier, Matt had helped the company launch an e-learning platform. The product struggled, but he stayed deep in the work, writing copy, managing partners, even staffing event booths. During that period, the CEO offered him a full-time Head of Sales role at $200,000 a year. Matt declined without hesitation. He didn't want a boss. He was already independent, running a real business with paying clients.

After the contract ended, the company was acquired by a major tech firm. The CEO then launched a venture fund and brought that Head of Sales in as a partner. That seat could have been Matt's.

The role would have paid his living costs while he gained experience within a scaling company. It came with access, context, and upside that only appeared later.

Instead, pride made the call. The cost was seven figures.

That moment changed how Matt thought about work. Employment wasn't a constraint. It was the capital.

Employment isn't Plan B. It's the foundation you build on.

The Value of the Job

A job is more than income. It is downside protection for your life. Steady cash flow covers fixed costs and extends your runway through healthcare, paid time off, and employer retirement contributions. It absorbs risk while you build leverage elsewhere.

Employment also gives you paid access to execution. You learn inside real systems, with real stakes, using tools and processes that are expensive to replicate on your own. You gain pattern recognition faster because mistakes are subsidized by the company, not your savings.

Finally, a job places you inside networks that matter. Customers, colleagues, and leaders often become future clients, partners, references, and deal flow. Many of the most valuable opportunities originate in rooms you were paid to be in.

For most people, employment income is the primary driver of wealth. In the United States, the majority of net worth is built through wages, salaries, and the skills and experience developed on the job—not from inheritance or passive investments.[5]

Three-Year Employment Runs

High-performing professionals see each job as a three-year tour of duty. Not a forever home, not a one-night stand: a contract worth roughly $300,000 of lifetime value. That's the price of a small house. You wouldn't buy a home without research, inspection, and negotiation, so don't take a job without the same diligence. Talk to people on the team, ask about leadership, growth paths, and product strength. You're not just accepting a paycheck; you're investing three years of your life.

This mindset also stabilizes your psychology. When you commit up front to a three-year window, you stop reacting emotionally to the first rough quarter or new manager. Year one is for developing foundational expertise and experience. Year two is for building on your progress. Year three is for maximizing compensation or preparing your next move. That rhythm keeps you locked in on execution instead of anxiety.

Each employment experience improves your skills, expands your network, and grows your net worth. Treat each one like a $300,000 asset, not a job title.

Engineering a $4M Career

Over a typical 40-year career, you may earn roughly $4M in total employment income—the equivalent of about 13 "runs" of $300,000 each.[6] If you consistently save and invest just 25% of those earnings, that alone can grow into a $1M exchange-traded fund portfolio.

Mission Brief: Generate $4M in earned income via employment.

Each role is a distinct earning period. Some will outperform expectations, others will fall short, but each should leave you more valuable than when you started. Employment is not one continuous stretch; it is a series of defined roles that together form your income base. That income base finances everything that follows.

Job searches feel uncertain when they lack structure. Resumes disappear into applicant tracking systems. Effort turns into guesswork. The advantage goes to people who run a repeatable process, where each step increases the odds of the next.

It starts with **Scouting**. Avoid broad outreach. Identify a short list of companies that match your skills, target compensation, and trajectory. Then map the people inside them: hiring managers, recruiters, and peers. The goal is context. Where is the business winning, where is it stuck, and where could you add value?

Next comes the **Signal**. A concise message. A short conversation. A thoughtful interaction. This is not a pitch. It is a demonstration of relevance. The objective is a response that creates a next step.

Then comes the **Handoff**. An internal referral, a resume forwarded, a name mentioned in the right room. You move from anonymous applicant to known candidate. That shift changes the process entirely.

The interview is **Execution**. You arrive informed. You understand the product, the customer, and the constraints. You tie answers to outcomes you've already delivered. The conversation stays focused on results, not personality.

Finally, the score. The **Offer**. This is where preparation shows. You review compensation, equity, benefits, flexibility, and growth. You negotiate from readiness, not urgency.

In a crowded job market, standing out is hard. The fastest way to rise above the noise is by earning internal referrals from your target companies. Job boards rarely work. Most applications vanish, and even when reviewed, recruiters often treat them as low priority.

An internal referral changes everything. It gives you instant credibility through a personal endorsement from someone inside the company who trusts your expertise. A single referral can move you from the bottom of the stack to the interview table.

Start by identifying employees at your target firms who can connect you to opportunities. If you do not have direct contacts, use LinkedIn to find people in similar departments. Ask for a brief informational interview to gain insight into the company and establish rapport.

Treat referrals like prospecting. Set weekly targets for outreach, calls, and introductions. Aim for one new internal referral each week. Track your numbers and adjust your strategy based on response rates.

Keep your messages short, professional, and specific. Show genuine interest in the company and explain how you can add value. At the end of each conversation, ask if they would consider referring you for the role.

Referrals come through relationships, not luck or applications.

2K to Pay Day

The average job search takes about four months and requires far more effort than most people expect.[7] From first outreach to final offer, the process can involve roughly 2,000 individual actions.

Prospecting turns into conversations. Conversations turn into referrals. Referrals turn into interviews. Interviews turn into offers. Every message, call, and connection is a rep that moves you closer to the goal. Consistency creates momentum, and momentum produces results.

Aim for 15 outreach activities a day through messages, comments, or introductions. Schedule one informational interview each week. Secure one or two referrals each month that lead to active interviews.

Over time, the ratios hold. About one in four informational interviews leads to a referral, and about one in two referrals results in a live interview. 2,000 actions, 1 offer, worth $300,000 over 3 years.

Matt's 5-Month Employment Search

Landing a new job in today's competitive economy was one of the hardest challenges Matt had ever faced.

Over five months, he applied to 92 jobs, conducted more than 20 informational interviews, participated in 13 formal interview processes, and received just one offer, which he accepted.

The mental and emotional toll was heavy. There was rejection, self-doubt, and worry about whether Matt would ever work again.

Coaching from David Ploshay, Aaron Ross, and his career coach helped him stay focused. David advised him to prioritize internal referrals and apply only when someone inside the company agreed to guide him through the process. Aaron provided introductions to sales leaders at companies like HubSpot and Samsara, which led to valuable calls and interviews. His career coach gave him the structure to organize the entire search.

Matt's sales background helped him with outreach, but he was underprepared for interviews. He realized most questions followed repeatable themes. Once he built strong base answers, he could tailor them to each company. He researched pain points, carefully studied job descriptions, and treated every rejection as practice.

At first, he aimed for big tech firms, but later turned his attention to smaller startups in his niche where his competencies fit directly. That adjustment made the difference.

The job he landed was not a household name, but it was the right fit: a role in his zone, with a team he respected, solving problems he cared about.

Modern job searches require more than a polished resume and LinkedIn profile. They reward patience and personal marketing skills that many professionals never develop.

Create Your Own Openings

Good roles are posted. They're also crowded. Hundreds of qualified applicants, little context, and no real advantage. In that market, credentials blur together and decisions come down to timing and luck.

The edge comes from having an angle. Every company is under pressure somewhere. Priorities stack up. Projects stall. Problems linger without owners. These gaps exist because teams are busy, budgets are fixed, and incentives don't line up. When you can spot one and articulate it clearly, you stop competing on paper and start competing on usefulness.

Start by studying companies in your lane. Look at how they sell, market, ship, and support customers. Notice friction. Slow handoffs. Confusing messaging. Leaky funnels. These signals point to work the company knows needs doing but hasn't staffed yet.

Once you see the gap, frame a solution. Keep it narrow. You're not proposing a reorg. You're showing that you understand the business and can move one metric. Revenue, growth, cost, or speed. Pick one. Explain how you'd approach it and what changes as a result.

Then reach out. Introduce yourself. Name the problem. Outline your approach. This isn't a job ask. It's a value demonstration.

Smaller companies tend to respond faster. Fewer layers. Less ceremony. If you show up with insight and a plan, you stand out immediately. Larger companies move slower, but the logic holds. When you can clearly define a real problem and speak to outcomes, you rise above the noise.

This flips the dynamic. You stop waiting to be selected. You create relevance. You move from applicant to participant.

Once you have the role, the goal is to get full value from it.

First, master your tools. Choose one core technology your team depends on and become an expert in it. Read the documentation, get certified, and share your knowledge online. Technical fluency makes you more valuable and more challenging to replace.

Second, use every benefit. Capture your full employer retirement match. Take advantage of health, insurance, and education perks. Use conference budgets and training stipends. These often-overlooked benefits can add up to thousands of dollars annually.

Third, push for upside. Do not limit negotiations to cash compensation. Equity, bonuses, title, role scope, and work flexibility often matter just as much. Make it a rule to counter at least one element of every annual compensation proposal. Most professionals accept the first version and move on. You treat each cycle as a review of the entire package.

Even the strongest professionals get blindsided. The issue isn't the hit itself, but rather being unprepared for it.

Getting fired or laid off is painful. It shakes your confidence and sense of identity. One week you are essential, the next you are forgotten. That shock can make people freeze or panic. The only way through is to advance quickly, hold tempo, and operate with structure. Start by managing what you can. Gather your documents, performance records, and any written feedback that proves your impact. Potentially file for unemployment benefits. Protect your cash. Tell a small circle of trusted peers what happened and look forward, not back.

Almost everyone gets fired at some point. It does not define you. It redirects you. Many endings turn out to be turning points. Shorten the emotional recovery and get back into motion fast. Momentum is key to rebuilding quickly.

If you sense trouble ahead, prepare before impact. Line up references, refresh your portfolio, and start conversations. If the layoff arrives without warning, negotiate before walking out. Do not accept the first offer. A calm discussion can extend income or benefits by weeks or months. Thank them for the opportunity, reiterate your contributions, and ask for better terms directly.

In the U.S. tech sector, the median severance package is roughly eight weeks of pay, though many receive less without negotiation.[8]

Contingencies are not just a defense; they are part of a durable, dynamic income strategy. Build a margin of safety: maintain a cash cushion, cultivate a strong network, and develop a portable track record. The goal is to be shock-resistant. When others stall, you adapt—because you already have options. That is strength under pressure.

Matt Makes $44K in 3 Months

Matt joined what he thought was a routine one-on-one meeting. Instead, both sales leaders were on the call. Within minutes, they told him he was being let go after only three months on the job.

He had been outperforming most of the team, closing deals and hitting targets. But the company wanted order-takers. They didn't want someone who thought. They wanted someone who obeyed.

The off-boarding email came next: two weeks of severance. Matt refused to accept it. He opened an AI writing tool, drafted a professional message, and made his case. He outlined his performance, teamwork, and the positive feedback he had received from leadership. Then he asked for three months of severance. Negotiate your offers, ask for annual raises, and secure your max severance.

The co-founder, who knew the situation had been mishandled, approved the request. Three months of severance. Secured.

By the end of Q1, Matt had already earned $44,000 in employment income. Even with the setback, he was still ahead of his annual target. He only needed another $56,000 to hit his $100,000 yearly employment income goal.

Moments like this reveal an important truth: we don't get what we deserve; we get what we ask for. Always negotiate your severance. Even if the answer is no, it costs nothing to ask, and every dollar matters when you have just been cut loose.

Even small negotiations compound like investments over time. Imagine two professionals who each start at $100,000 a year, at age 25 and work until 65. One follows the standard track, accepting 3% raises each year. The other earns 5% annual increases through consistent negotiation, strong performance, and well-timed career moves.

After 40 years, the difference adds up. The standard path produces about $7.5M in total earnings, while the more proactive path reaches roughly $12.1M. That is a $4.6M gap created entirely by asking for more.

Each raise compounds on the one before it. What looks incremental in the moment, becomes decisive over time, often marking the line between treading water and long-term security.

The $500,000 Employment Operator

David built his income like a professional, not a dreamer. He focused on one of the most lucrative paths for non-engineers: enterprise sales.[9]

Over time, he thrived across multiple tech companies, advancing into roles with access to larger deal sizes while sharpening his soft skills along the way. His philosophy was simple and executable: intentionality. He deliberately chose remote-friendly sales roles that weren't constrained by geography or limited to local territories.

Sales rewards lifelong learning, grit, and consistency. Rather than chasing titles or startup bets, he committed to the 10,000-hour approach of becoming a top individual contributor at established organizations. He studied his craft and refined his value proposition, eventually targeting only firms that he verified had multiple people in his same role earning above $500K annually. That strategy paid off—David crossed the $500K mark. He channels the surplus into Vanguard ETFs, letting his portfolio grow toward seven figures.

David's job searches have mirrored his sales process. Influenced by *Predictable Revenue* and refined through a relationship with Matt A. Smith and Aaron Ross, he built a repeatable process for landing elite roles. He leverages referrals, treats hiring managers like prospects, and cultivates a circle of peers and mentors for feedback and accountability.

For David, employment is not just income. It is the base of his entire financial strategy. A strong sales career funds the capital for a robust liquid financial investment portfolio.

13 tours. $4M in earned income. That is the baseline.

Most people drift through employment without intention and never extract its full value. You treat each role as a defined tour, with a target, a timeline, and an outcome.

Commit to your employer for a tour of duty. Then use the surplus to build your next income stream: freelancing.

CHAPTER 4: FREELANCE OS

"When someone pays for your judgment, you're in business."

— Alan Weiss

The resort in Mexico felt like a dream: wristbands on, margaritas in hand, and friends drifting between pools and beach bars. It was James Leonardo's wedding week, the kind of celebration that made life feel whole and complete. He was a tech executive with a substantial salary and a promising career path. Everything looked solid on paper.

One night after dinner on the beach, his best friend Matt pulled him aside and said, "James, you're not even in the game." The words struck a chord, but it was true. James had a career, but no control over it. The moment his paycheck stopped, so would everything he'd built.

When James returned home to Las Vegas, he decided to change that. Without a website or logo, he opened his laptop and started reaching out to people who already trusted him.

Within a few weeks, he landed his first client. Six months later, he had earned $50,000 working about 20 hours a week.

That project gave him newfound confidence and a sense of ownership he hadn't felt before. Today, with his wife and growing family, James runs a freelancing business designed to support him for decades.

Mission Brief: Build a freelance income source that delivers six figures annually and $4M in lifetime earnings.

Freelancing provides a direct and flexible path to financial freedom. You operate without investors, inventory, or high upfront costs. You use the talents you already have, turn them into a service, and deliver results for businesses that will benefit. Each project becomes a feedback loop of action and adjustment.

Freelancing isn't about big bets. It's a measured approach to entrepreneurship with low costs, strong margins, and time to evolve as you build. The question isn't whether you can do this. It's whether you're ready to start.

Model this across a 40-year career. The goal is $4M in total freelance income, not revenue. To get there, the business needs to generate roughly $6M in total revenue at a 65% profit margin. That works out to about $150,000 in annual revenue, producing around $100,000 in pre-tax operating income.

Here's what that looks like in practice. A client paying $5,000 a month, retained for six months, generates $30,000. Land five engagements like that in a year, and you've hit $150,000 in revenue, right on target. Five client cycles a year is the engine. Not fifty clients. Five solid engagements, repeated consistently.

Prefer to think in time? At $200 an hour, hitting $150,000 a year requires about 60 billable hours a month, roughly 15 a week. Focused evenings, deliberate weekend blocks. It fits inside a real schedule.

This is arithmetic, not optimism. Most jobs end earlier than people expect. When that happens, skills alone don't pay the bills. You need a way to turn that proficiency into income. That's what freelancing really is. Not a side hustle or a backup plan. A small, solid business that sits next to your job and often lasts longer than it.

Two common misconceptions distort freelancing: one sees it as a short-term cash grab, and the other as a quick path to wealth. Both miss the point. Freelancing works best when it's boring, repeatable, and reliable.

Don't wait for the right idea or the right moment. Businesses don't start that way. Begin small, sell existing expertise, and improve through repetition.

The approach is simple and unglamorous. Offer what you already know. Charge for it. Deliver consistently. Retain your clients. Repeat.

Unlike startups, freelancing doesn't depend on luck or external funding. Unlike jobs, it rarely disappears overnight. It usually ends only when you stop running it.

That's why it belongs in your forever income portfolio.

If possible, start freelancing while keeping your day job. This is not disloyalty; it's a calculated strategy. Your salary provides cash flow while your side work builds your entrepreneurial toolkit.

Keep your lanes separate. Never use company devices, accounts, or time for outside work. That includes laptops, email, and internal tools. Treat your freelance projects as a completely different business.

Read your contract. Know what clauses exist around outside work, non-compete, and intellectual property. Most employers permit freelancing provided it does not overlap or interfere with work. If something seems restrictive, seek legal advice before proceeding.

Avoid conflicts of interest. Do not take clients that compete with your employer or use inside information. Protect both your reputation and your primary source of employment income.

Set up a clean structure. Create a standard legal entity, one bank account, and one record system. Keep taxes organized and your business separate from personal finances. It signals professionalism and makes expansion easier later.

Moonlighting builds economic security and resilience; it's not an act of rebellion against your employer. It's a hedge that creates income control long before a crisis appears. Waiting for disruption is a mistake. Start early and build from a stable base, not desperation.

Closing a freelance client feels impossible until it happens. All it takes is one person with a problem and the confidence to say, "I can help."

Who already knows what you can do? Former coworkers, classmates, and friends are more likely to seek your help than strangers. A quick message offering support on a small project can open the door. Start the conversation. Freelancing begins with connection, not marketing.

Matt was living in Marina del Rey, trying to revive a failing e-commerce idea, when a former colleague mentioned his name to a startup looking for sales help. Within three days, he was sitting on Hollywood Boulevard, coffee in hand, watching the tourists and street performers while waiting for the CEO. By the end of that meeting, he had a consulting gig. No firm, no brand, no plan. Just experience, trust, and timing.

That initial project paid $5,000 a month and gave him something more important than income: validation. Once you have been paid for your expertise, you realize you can do it again. From there, opportunities multiply. Within weeks, Matt used that experience to land a stronger client, a remote consulting role that fit his proficiency and values. His freelance story began not with a business plan, but with a coffee and a conversation.

Freelancing follows a simple three-step loop: connect, listen, and offer. Send a message through email, text, or LinkedIn. Listen before you sell. Ask what they are working on and where they are stuck. If you see a gap you can fill, make a specific offer.

Find alignment. A good client relationship begins when both sides understand the problem and believe the partnership makes sense. That mutual understanding matters more than any detailed proposal.

Once there is alignment, outline what success looks like in plain language. Define the outcome, deliverables, timeline, and price. Keep it short enough to fit on one page. This is not about legal protection yet. It is about shared understanding. When both sides agree on the outcome, projects run smoothly and trust grows faster.

Client one is not the final version of your business. It is the first draft. Many professionals never start because they think they must have everything figured out first. The opposite is true. You figure it out by engaging with the market. You refine as you go. One $20,000 client this month. Four more by year-end. $100,000 total.

Aaron Narrows His Niche

After leaving Salesforce, Aaron hit what he called "business identity confusion." He didn't want to do more sales consulting. He wanted something new, something meaningful. So he tried everything. Coaching. Writing a book. Hosting workshops. Blogging. Posting videos. A little traction here, a little money there, but nothing that lasted.

Every week felt like starting over from scratch. Aaron was attempting to run five businesses at once instead of focusing on one that could succeed. He had the skills, but not the focus. Bills piled up, and "figuring it out" stopped being optional.

When his family grew, the pressure became intense. He sought financial security, and that urgency forced him to make a choice. He stopped chasing new ideas and went back to what he already knew: outbound sales. It wasn't glamorous, but it was his proven specialty. Companies were looking for it, and he was good at it.

He went all in. Partnered with someone who shared his vision. Built a proper website. Published a book on sales. Within months, demand took off. He raised his workshop prices, then raised them again. The business finally clicked. $10M in freelance income followed.

The thing he had been avoiding was the thing that worked best. Customers buy solutions from consultants with experience, not potential.

You don't plan your way into a niche. You spend years executing in it. So pick one problem and solve it for one type of person. Test and watch what happens in the marketplace. When it works, repeat. When it doesn't, adjust. Every failure gives you data for the next iteration.

Your first focus likely won't be the one you stick with long-term. That's fine. Traction over perfection. Being understandable is your best marketing. When people instantly know who you help and how, they either hire you or refer someone who will.

Ideal businesses only exist on paper. Start the messy one now that resonates with actual customers.

The Warm Network Advantage

Every great freelance business is built on relationships. Not algorithms. Not ads. People.

Many new freelancers waste months perfecting websites, content strategies, or funnels instead of focusing on relationships. Your first five clients won't come from marketing. They'll come from direct outreach.

The fastest path to opportunity is through people who already know, like, and trust you. Friends, coworkers, mentors, and former bosses. These are your first-degree connections. They'll either hire you or introduce you to someone who will.

Trust works like distance: the closer someone is to you, the less effort it takes to convince them. The farther away your clients are, the harder you have to work. That's why your priority should be on the people nearest to your network. Warm introductions open doors that cold emails can't.

Reaching out to your network doesn't have to feel awkward. Keep it basic: "Hey, I'm doing some consulting on [proficiency]. Do you know anyone who might benefit from help with that?"

Over time, these interactions become your pipeline. Each one teaches you how people describe their problems and what they're willing to pay to solve them. It's how you master the language of your market.

The modern world is noisy and full of automation. Everyone is trying to scale faster. That makes genuine connections more valuable than ever. When people trust you, they stop comparing prices and start prioritizing your availability. That trust turns one project into ongoing business, referrals, and reliable income.

Grow your business one relationship at a time. The cumulative effect is substantial. A few strong connections today can generate years of freelance revenue tomorrow.

Top freelancers don't rely on visibility. They rely on relationships that produce referrals and repeat business behind the scenes.

The Discovery Call

Your first sales conversation is a diagnostic, not a pitch. You're there to uncover problems, clarify outcomes, and determine fit. Persuasion is not the goal.

Sales isn't about putting on a show; it's about understanding the client's needs through thorough research. Your job is to uncover what matters most to the person in front of you. Identify the pain, clarify the objective, and determine if this is someone you want to work with.

You're qualifying them as much as they're qualifying you. Good clients value expertise and decisiveness. Weak clients negotiate on price alone. The conversation reveals which one you're talking to. Ask questions, listen closely, and take notes. The more they talk, the more you learn.

When you describe your approach, be direct. Speak to outcomes, not deliverables. Don't say "I'll run a 12-week content strategy." Say "I'll help you generate 50 qualified leads per month through LinkedIn." People buy results, not process. Show that you understand the problem and have a plan to solve it.

When it comes to pricing, be direct. State the number, pause, and let them respond. If they push back on price before understanding scope, that's a signal. Strong clients negotiate on terms and outcomes. Weak clients negotiate on rate alone.

Every call should end with a clear next step: a proposal, a follow-up meeting, or a mutual decision to pass. Ambiguity kills deals.

Most projects fail before they start. Not from bad work, but from fuzzy agreements. A success agreement is five questions on one page.

What problem exists? What gets delivered? How do we measure success? When is it done? What does it cost?

Answer all five. Write them down. Get both signatures. That's the agreement. No legal jargon. No twelve-page contracts. No clauses drafted by attorneys who've never done the work. Just clear language that states what happens, when it happens, and what it costs.

The agreement protects both sides. You know exactly what you're delivering. They know exactly what they're getting. When scope creep appears (and it will), you point to the page. When timelines slip, the document resets expectations. When invoices go out, there's no confusion about what was agreed to.

Write it before you start. Most consultants negotiate verbally, shake hands, and assume everyone remembers the same conversation. They don't. Memory is selective. Pressure distorts details. Three weeks in, "I thought you were handling X" becomes a problem. The success agreement eliminates that.

If a client resists putting it in writing, that's your answer. Professional engagements begin with documentation. Amateurs wing it and hope for the best. Skip the twenty-slide deck. Skip the proposal template with stock photos. A success agreement can live in an email, a PDF, or a Google Doc. Format doesn't matter. Clarity does.

Once both sides sign, start the work. The agreement stays visible throughout the project. Reference it in updates. Tie deliverables back to it. When the project closes, compare results to what was promised.

That's how professionals operate. Clear terms. Documented outcomes. No surprises.

Get It in Writing

Matt got the call from a friend he trusted. A mentor who ran an innovative agency that did marketing work for big telecom clients. The offer sounded easy. Jump in, help the team, and get a $7,000 monthly retainer. It felt like a win all around, meaningful money, good people, no red tape.

The work started immediately. The team looped Matt into calls, shared files, and gave him deliverables. Everything moved as if he were already under contract, except for one problem. The contract didn't exist. The end client, a bloated telecom company with too many layers of approval, kept dragging its feet. Every time Matt asked about paperwork, he got the same line: the contract is still being reviewed by the legal office, and should be signed any day now. Keep working.

Three months later, the company owed Matt $21,000. Still no signature. The project had gone live, positive outcomes delivered, and now his patience was gone. Matt told the telecom he would stop work unless they paid. They finally sent a check. This was not a step forward; it was a warning.

Another three months went by. Still no paperwork. Another $21,000 on the line. This time, the tone changed. The telecom client canceled the contract. Matt's mentor friend stopped replying. The calls went unanswered. Matt had been ghosted by a friend, burned by a client, and was left holding the bag.

$21,000 vanished into corporate fog. The sting wasn't just about the money. It was the realization that goodwill means nothing without signatures. That lesson never faded. Get the paper signed. Get paid before you deliver.

Finding More Clients

Landing one client proves the concept; finding the next few turns freelancing into a business. Closing and delivering for 200 clients leads to $4M in personal income. The challenge is consistency. Many freelancers ride a cycle of feast and famine because they treat client work like luck. Not you. You keep generating consistent opportunities and conversations.

Client acquisition runs on two tracks: reactivation and expansion.

Reactivation means going back to past clients with new offers. The easiest sale is to someone who's already hired you once. Follow up quarterly. Ask what's changed. Propose the next engagement before they think to look elsewhere.

Expansion means growing your circle. Join communities and networks where your ideal clients spend time. Contribute specific insights from client work. Answer questions other consultants avoid. Demonstrate expertise through what you've already solved, not what you could theoretically do.

A massive audience isn't essential. What matters is a small group of people who know you deliver. Find them through outreach. Keep them through results.

Don't rely on inbound leads to save your business. Inbound is earned and rare in the solo freelancer game. Outbound is controlled. Keep initiating. Keep following up. Most deals close after multiple touches, not one.

Even if you start getting regular work, keep prospecting anyway. The best time to establish your pipeline is when you have no immediate use for it. That discipline prevents panic later.

Freelancers who master client acquisition never worry about where the next invoice will come from. They know that every project creates another signal of competence. Each result attracts the next opportunity.

You are not chasing clients. You are building a client acquisition machine that can be sustained.

Freelancer marketing fails because it chases visibility instead of memory. Reach does not get you hired. Recall does.

Clients don't scroll, compare, and choose the best post. They remember one or two people when a problem arises. The job goes to whoever is already top of mind.

Memory is built through repeated exposure in a single context. When your ideas, voice, and results show up in the same place over time, your name becomes linked to a specific problem. That association is an asset.

Posting everywhere breaks that link. Each platform resets context, audience, and expectations. You stay visible but forgettable.

One channel works because it trains recognition. Same format. Same audience. Same angle. Over time, people stop reading and start recognizing. That is when messages turn into introductions and referrals.

This is why consistency matters. Not for the algorithm, but for human memory. Every appearance reinforces a single mental slot. Miss enough weeks and you fall out of it.

Measure success by recall events. "I see you everywhere." "I thought of you." "Someone told me to talk to you." Those phrases mean the marketing is working.

Attention is not earned by being loud. It is earned by being remembered for one thing, in one place, long enough that your name becomes the default answer.

The 100:10:1 Method

If you want a six-figure freelance income, prospecting has to be a core ability. The bottleneck isn't talent or quality of work. It's the absence of a repeatable sales process that produces clients on schedule.

Your next $100,000 year is sitting inside 1,000 messages. The equation is simple: 100 outreaches create 10 conversations, and 10 conversations lead to one win.

Tactical Tip: Execute one freelancing sales conversation every week.

Predictable freelancing revenue stems from tracking your efforts. Until then, you're guessing. Most freelancers reach out to 10 prospects and wonder why nothing happens. They post something online and wait for clients to appear. The ones who win treat outreach like breathing.

The 100:10:1 funnel provides a simple baseline for prospecting: 100 messages, 10 meaningful conversations, and one paying client.[10] The ratios are consistent. If you're not closing, it's not because freelancing doesn't work—it's because you stopped before the numbers had time to pay out.

Do this once and you'll get a taste of it. Repeat the process ten times to establish a $100,000 base. No complicated funnels or viral posts needed.

To run it, start by writing down 100 names. People you can help. Companies in your space. Past coworkers. Warm connections first, cold ones later. Execute high-volume outreach into the warm network.

The best freelancers are not the most talented. They are the most persistent. They understand that every yes is buried under a pile of ignored messages.

The 100:10:1 method turns freelancing from mystery into muscle memory. It's not a theory. It's arithmetic.

Once you have a few projects under your belt, it is time to define your model. Not your brand or logo, but the structure behind how you earn, deliver, and get seen.

In the service industry, the titles vary. Consultant. Coach. Contractor. Advisor. Fractional executive. Freelancer. The label matters less than how you work and how you get paid.

At one end, you execute. You design, write, build, or manage the project yourself. This is the contractor model. Clients pay for outcomes. It pays quickly, builds skill fast, and earns credibility. The tradeoff is time. When you stop working, income pauses too.

On the other end, you're a guide. You teach, advise, and help others make better decisions. This is the advisor model. It scales better, offers more flexibility, and builds lasting relationships. But it also takes credibility, trust, and patience to sell.

Most professionals live in the middle. They blend strategy with execution. They start hands-on, then evolve toward higher-value guidance as experience grows.

Your model is not a title. It is the method for turning abilities into repeatable income.

The Service Selector

Freelancers execute services. Yes, but what services exactly? This grid shows you what to sell, how to price it, and how your offers connect. Stop relying on guesswork to shape your services. Design them with purpose. The Service Selector measures time on one side and earning potential on the other. Move up over time toward higher value, higher leverage work.

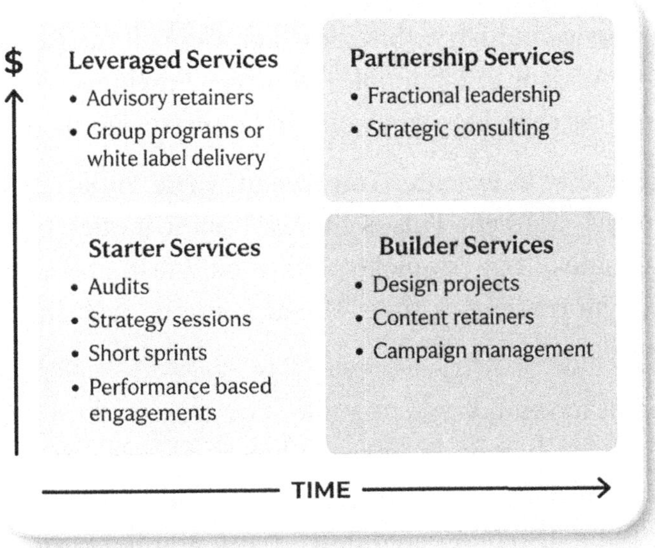

The Service Selector

Starter Services sit in the bottom left. These are quick, low-commitment offers that open the relationship and reduce friction for a first engagement. Examples include audits, strategy sessions, short sprints, and performance-based engagements tied to clearly defined outcomes such as leads generated, meetings booked, or deals won. These structures shift risk away from the client and make it easier to say yes early. A $1,000 audit might uncover a $10,000 project. A performance-based engagement might convert into a monthly retainer once trust is established. Starter Services are where proof is created, expectations are set, and the upsell path begins.

Builder Services live in the bottom right. These are hands-on projects such as campaign management, design retainers, go-to-market services, or content development. They require consistent time and execution. Clients pay for output and visible progress, often between $2,500 and $7,500 per month. This stage helps you develop talents, processes, and results you can show. It builds credibility but can also become a bottleneck if you remain in this phase indefinitely.

Leveraged Services sit in the top left. These include advisory retainers, group programs, or subcontracted white-label delivery. They allow you to serve more clients without adding more hours. A leveraged offer might be a monthly advisory retainer that includes structured calls, private feedback, and access to your frameworks. These models earn $5,000 to $15,000 per month. They trade direct labor for scale and margin.

Partnership Services occupy the top right. These are high-trust, high-value engagements where you operate as a senior individual contributor, coach, or strategic lead. This can include high-level coaching, strategy consulting, or top-tier execution such as serving as a fractional head of a function or owning a critical initiative. You are paid for analysis, decisions, and outcomes, not hours or task lists. The work may involve building an annual plan, setting direction for a team, or directly running a business unit with full accountability. Fees typically range from $10,000 to $30,000 or more per month, reflecting the scope, responsibility, and impact of the role.

The Service Selector is more than a pricing model. It is a value ladder and roadmap for growth. Starter Services establish trust and seamlessly pave the way for Builder projects. Builder projects create results that evolve into Leveraged or Partnership work. Each step gives you stronger positioning and higher margins. Over time, your offers form a connected path that grows your income while reducing how much time you spend earning it.

The Two-Offer Strategy

Most freelancers struggle with pricing because they try to sell too many things at once. Offering too many services creates confusion for buyers. Complexity slows decisions.

Start with two offers only. A Project and a Partnership. Together, they create a clear entry point, a logical upgrade path, and a freelance business that is easier to explain, sell, and repeat.

A Project is a short-term engagement built around one specific technology. Salesforce. HubSpot. Zendesk. ChatGPT. Not broad promises like “sales optimization” or “AI strategy,” but a defined intervention tied to a single platform with a visible outcome. A pipeline rebuild, a support workflow redesign, or an internal AI deployment.

Limiting a Project to one technology tightens scope and sharpens positioning. Your content, credentials, and case studies can all point to mastery of that system. Over time, you become top of mind for that tool because everything you publish and deliver reinforces the same message.

Projects are fast and concrete, usually lasting between two weeks and three months. They are typically priced as fixed-fee engagements in the $3,000 to $15,000 range, depending on scope and system depth. Their purpose is to create trust through results, not to solve everything at once. When the technology and outcome are clear, pricing becomes simpler and confidence rises on both sides.

The Partnership builds from that foundation.

A Partnership is an ongoing strategic role layered on the same technology. You step into a defined seat inside the business, such as Head of Customer Support with deep Zendesk expertise or a revenue leader responsible for Salesforce. The client is buying senior judgment applied consistently over time.

Partnerships are typically structured as monthly retainers ranging from $5,000 to $20,000, depending on scope, responsibility, and decision authority. The fee reflects access to leadership and accountability, not volume of work.

Pricing stabilizes because it anchors to the cost of a full-time leader with the same skill set. The Partnership becomes a practical alternative to hiring, rather than a discounted consulting arrangement.

The client's decision becomes straightforward. If they want a fast, contained result, they start with a Project. If they want ongoing leadership and accountability, they move into a Partnership. You always know what to propose, and the buyer understands what they are buying.

This structure strengthens over time. Specializing in one technology defines your niche and sharpens your message. Layering that expertise into a strategic role turns short-term wins into durable revenue. Two offers are enough to build a repeatable predictable freelance business that can scale to six-figures in annual income.

Metrics That Matter

Freelancers fall into two traps: dashboard overload or flying blind. You do not need a complex dashboard to run a freelance business. A small set of numbers tells you whether your pipeline is producing real opportunities, whether deals are converting, and whether clients are likely to stick around.

The first metric is **conversations**. One-on-one discussions with potential clients about real problems. No conversations means nothing else matters. If this number is low, the issue is not pricing or positioning. It is outreach.

Next are **qualified opportunities**. These are prospects with a defined problem, urgency, and budget. Track how many exist at any given time. If conversations are happening but opportunities are not forming, your targeting or offer structure is off.

Then comes **win rate**. The percentage of qualified opportunities that turn into paying clients. This reveals trust and how well your offer is understood. A low win rate usually means your scope, pricing, or message is muddy. A strong win rate means buyers recognize the value quickly.

Deal size comes next. This is the value of a single engagement at the moment a client says yes. One project. One retainer start. Deal size reflects positioning and pricing confidence. A $5,000 project vs. a $25,000 engagement is rarely about five times more work. It's about how the problem is framed. If your wins are consistently small, the issue is rarely volume. It is how the work is framed and scoped at the entry point.

Finally, **lifetime value**. This measures how much revenue a client generates over the entire relationship. Initial work, follow-on projects, renewals, and expansions all count. Lifetime value shows whether clients want to keep you involved after the first success. If deal size is healthy but lifetime value is low, the issue is retention and progression, not pricing.

Each of these numbers answers a different question. Together, they show where effort is being wasted and where improvement is possible. That is what turns freelancing from reactive work into a business you can reason about and improve deliberately.

Double Your Deal Size

Don't try to earn more by just adding clients. A better approach is to make each client worth more over time. Deal size grows with ownership of outcomes, not effort. The path follows a predictable pattern: single, double, triple, home run.

The first stage is the single. a short pilot designed to prove competence and build trust. A 90-day engagement at $5,000 tied to a specific outcome. The purpose is to land the client and open the door to a longer relationship.

The second stage is the double. Once trust is established, the scope expands and accountability increases. The timeline extends to six months. Pricing moves to $10,000 or more. You are no longer testing ideas. You are responsible for results across a defined area.

Larger deals come from taking responsibility for a defined outcome, not from offering more tasks. A freelancer who helps with marketing gets small contracts. A freelancer who owns the quarterly marketing plan, the CRM rollout, or the customer support function gets larger ones. Deal size grows with ownership of outcomes.

The third stage is the triple. Accountability becomes explicit. You are running a function, not delivering projects. Pricing reflects that responsibility, often as a monthly retainer. The client is paying for ongoing decisions, prioritization, and results.

Occasionally, you **hit a home run**. This is a large, long-term engagement where you operate as a senior leader inside the business. These deals are rare, but they only appear when the earlier stages exist.

To increase deal size, design your offers for doubles and triples, not singles. If you only swing for singles, you will keep landing singles. When you scope and propose for larger outcomes from the start, those deals begin to appear. Larger deals do not arrive by accident. They show up when your offers, timelines, and accountability are built for them from the beginning.

Keeping clients is not about likability or loyalty. It is about structure, position, and how exits are handled. Freelancers risk losing clients when they are perceived as optional support rather than indispensable contributors.

Start with deal structure. Short projects end because they are designed to end. Longer relationships come from long-term agreements or performance-based engagements that tie your work to ongoing outcomes. When compensation is linked to results over time, the relationship naturally continues.

Next is strategic fit. Churn drops when you own a core function instead of a task list. Consultants who support marketing or assist with operations are easy to remove. Consultants who own the CRM, the quarterly plan, the support workflow, or a revenue function become harder to replace. The closer your work is to a core function, the more embedded you become.

Retention hinges on how visible and impactful your contributions are. Communication is not about being friendly. It is about reporting, framing, and explanation. Clients churn when they do not understand what they are paying for. Regular updates, simple reporting, and clear explanation of outcomes reduce uncertainty.

Be proactive about renewal. Sixty days before a project ends, talk about what comes next. Offer follow-up support, maintenance, or a deeper engagement. Do not wait for clients to reach out. Silence is the first stage of churn.

When a client signals they may leave, respond directly. Ask why. If the concern is budget, offer a temporary rate adjustment to preserve continuity. If the concern is results, narrow the scope and attach a clear outcome with a guarantee or money-back provision. The goal is not to defend past work. It is to reset expectations and keep momentum.

Clients leave when you are easy to remove. Make retention the default by owning outcomes, staying visible, and proposing what comes next before the work ends.

When Freelancing Opens Doors

During the lockdown, Matt was running his consulting business from a rental overlooking downtown San Diego. It looked ideal, but the rent was high and cash was tight. He needed new work fast.

Scrolling through LinkedIn one night, he spotted a post from a founder he respected who had just raised significant funding. Matt reached out, offered help, and soon landed a three-month consulting contract at $10,000 a month. It was the deal that kept him afloat.

Once inside the company, progress halted. The sales team resisted change. Instead of forcing ideas, Matt pivoted. He noticed the marketing was weak and started sending short reports to the founder, highlighting issues and solutions.

Those updates built trust. The founder began seeing Matt as a problem solver, not a consultant passing through. Within months, Matt transitioned into a marketing role and eventually joined the company full-time in a position that had not existed before. Over two years, that opportunity earned him more than $300,000.

None of it was planned. It happened because Matt stayed helpful, adaptable, and consistent. Freelancing gave him the leverage to create opportunities rather than waiting for them to appear.

That is the hidden power of freelancing. It creates doors that open only when you start moving.

The Differentiator

Employment and investing are common. Most professionals you know already do both in some form. Freelancing is the differentiator. The move from participant to triple threat operator.

This is where your identity changes. You stop being only an employee who executes inside one company and an investor who places small chips in other people's companies. You become a freelance entrepreneur who can create income on demand via your own business.

Freelancing is one of the fastest ways to accelerate income growth and build scalability that traditional employment often lacks. Raises are slow and scarce. Portfolios compound over years, not months. A strategically executed consulting engagement can generate an additional $60,000 to $100,000 annually.

Five clients per year. About $150,000 in revenue. Roughly $100,000 in income. Fifteen focused hours per week. Sustained for decades.

Freelancing abilities make your career more resilient. Once you earn through your own initiative, risk shrinks. You gain career leverage.

Most professionals already have a paycheck and a brokerage account. Adding a forever-freelance engine makes the trinity whole.

Freelancing is the keystone. Establish it once. Keep it alive. Let it fund what comes next: Investments.

CHAPTER 5: INVESTING OS

"Never depend on a single income.
Make investments to create a second source."

— Warren Buffett

Matt stared at the screen in his Coronado apartment, a little stunned. A year earlier, he was freelancing out of coffee shops, chasing invoices, and stacking projects just to cover rent. Then one client turned into a full-time offer with benefits and an employer-sponsored retirement account. For the first time, he could automate his investing instead of guessing with leftovers. Every paycheck sent about $1,500 into the S&P fund, the company matched, and the market did its work.

In just one year, the balance grew from $0 to $40,000. Not theory. Not luck. Capital to investments to returns. Freelancing had opened the opportunity. Employment with benefits and matching further monetized it. Investing in the right asset in the correct account multiplied the result and delivered a wealth boost.

He sat back and realized this was just the warm-up. The game was scale. You push for the bigger job, the better match, the higher stakes. The framework worked once. Now it was time to scale it: harder, faster, and bigger, until capital outpaced effort.

The Ownership Outcome

Every income architect reaches this point. You master your craft, increase your earnings, and grow a small services business. Yet your income still relies on your attention. You are capped.

You earn through work, you grow through mastery, and you expand through ownership. Investing isn't just about building wealth; it's about keeping pace with the world around you.

Over the past 30 years, the S&P 500 has delivered an average annual return of roughly 10%, while typical savings accounts have returned less than 1%.[11] Since 2000, inflation has reduced purchasing power by more than 40%, meaning $100 then buys less than $60 today.[12] Yet only about 58% of Americans own stocks at all, and the median portfolio is just $40,000.[13]

If your money isn't working for you, time is working against you. Every year you wait makes it harder to catch up.

Mission Brief: Accumulate $2.5M in fully liquid assets. A 4% withdrawal gives you $100,000 a year.

Investing is the pivot. It is the move from earning to owning, from effort-driven income to asset-driven income. This is not gambling or chasing trends. It is acquiring productive assets.

The Persistent Investor

Eric earned $165,000 annually as a product manager at a software company. No equity windfalls. No big bonuses. Just a regular salary and demanding weeks. Early on, he made one choice that shaped the rest of his financial life: he set aside 17% of every paycheck for investments. Most of it went into two broad, low-cost index ETFs, VTI for the United States market and VXUS for international. He automated everything and kept his routine simple.

Though his income stayed nearly flat for years, his investment accounts steadily grew. After eight years, his portfolio crossed $290,000. That number didn't put him ahead of anyone's perfect timeline. It reflected the early stage, when growth starts slowly before it begins to climb. This progress wasn't the result of clever trades; it came from sticking to a disciplined plan. When his company announced cuts, Eric realized something important. His role was uncertain, but his financial base had finally stabilized.

By year ten, that foundation changed how he operated. He approached new roles without rushing. He evaluated opportunities with a clear head. He moved to a better city for his career and negotiated without urgency. Nothing dramatic happened in his portfolio. This conventional, unglamorous strategy gave him financial options he had never experienced earlier in his career.

Cash Flow Discipline

Who has your millions of dollars? Employers and freelance clients have your money. We need to go get it. Every dollar you earn has a role. Income Operators direct, guide, and automate the flow.

Your income should hit two buckets, not twelve. One personal, one professional. From there, every dollar follows the same flow: earn, protect, invest, grow.

If you work for an employer, your salary is deposited into a personal checking account. That is your power center. Money first moves to eliminate high-interest debt, then into your investing account, where it starts to grow. You do not have to think about it each month. It runs on its own.

If you work for yourself, the sequence begins inside your business. Revenue lands in your business checking account. Expenses are cleared through a single card so you can track everything cleanly. You pay yourself a fixed salary from that account, just like an employee. From there, the same waterfall runs its course. Debts disappear, reserves grow, investments get funded.

The structure never changes. Core accounts. Automated transfers. Defined order.

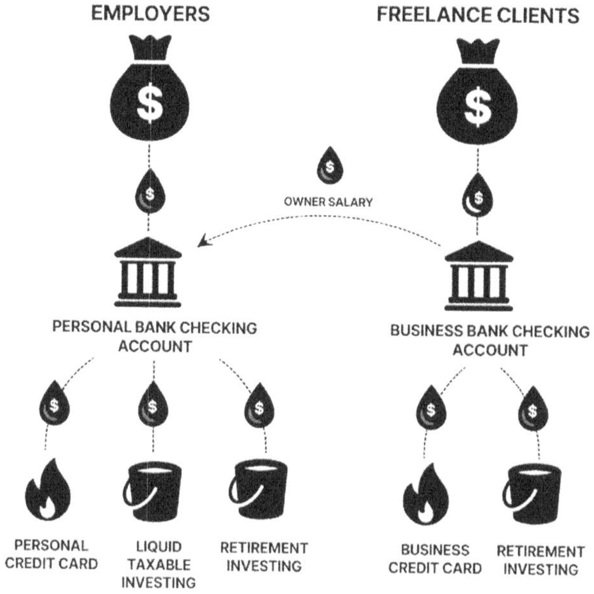

Wealth Waterfall

You don't need more complexity. You need flow discipline. With the wealth waterfall in place, building economic security becomes routine.[14] You earn, the system directs your money, and your assets grow automatically.

Accounts That Matter

Once the waterfall is flowing, we need to direct it into the proper buckets. That is where the pyramid comes in. Your investing life rests on three layers, each with a different purpose. Together, they create a balance between flexibility today and financial freedom tomorrow.

The foundation of the pyramid is your **liquid taxable brokerage account**, where you build tangible wealth. There are no contribution limits and no waiting periods. You can invest in public markets, funds, or even digital assets. Liquidity is power. It gives you the flexibility to seize opportunities, handle surprises, and move fast when others hesitate.

Above that sits your **personal retirement account**. Contributions may reduce your taxable income today, and returns grow without being taxed each year. Depending on how your account is structured, taxes are either deferred until withdrawal or avoided entirely. Either way, eliminating annual tax drag meaningfully accelerates wealth building over decades.

At the top sits the **employer-sponsored plan**. This is the hidden accelerator. When your employer offers a contribution match, you are being handed free money. That match, plus higher contribution limits, can supercharge your net worth over time.

These three layers work together. The liquid brokerage account provides agility. The personal retirement account builds safety. The employer plan multiplies your savings through matching. You do not need to obsess over every acronym or regulation. Just know which layer you are building and why.

A strong pyramid is broad at the base and stable at the top. The same rule applies here. Allow your accessible wealth to grow while your retirement and employer accounts appreciate over time. That balance is what makes this a great pyramid that can weather the sandstorms to come.

Once your accounts are in place, what you own inside them sets the cycle in motion. This is your Asset Blueprint, a structure that moves money through a deliberate sequence: income becomes capital, capital produces returns, returns are reinvested, and wealth accumulates. Each allocation has a defined role: liquidity for protection, broad market funds for steady growth, and direct ownership for long-term upside.

ETFs should make up roughly 40% of your portfolio, forming the foundation for sustained growth. One trade gives you exposure to hundreds of companies while keeping costs low. Start broad with total market or S&P 500 funds, automate contributions, and let consistency drive results.

Above that sits 20% in money market funds—your consistent yield slice. This is where your cash begins to earn. Instead of leaving it idle in a checking account at near-zero returns, you move it here and earn 4% to 5% with minimal volatility.[15]

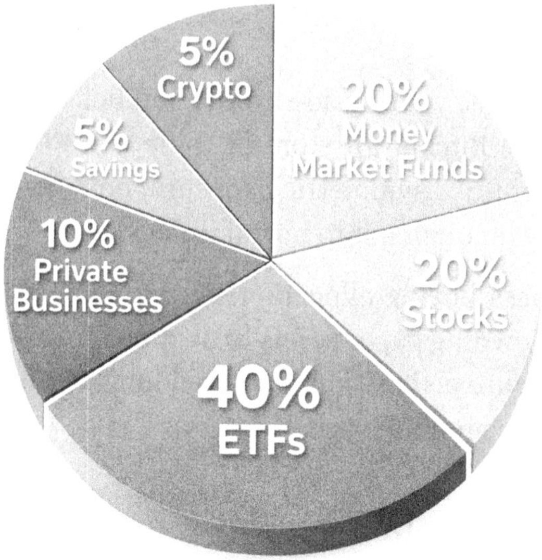

The Asset Blueprint

Next is 20% in individual stocks, your upside slice. Once your foundation is solid, direct ownership becomes your edge. This is where insights turn into returns. Buy companies you understand, hold them through cycles, and let results, not headlines, prove you right.

Individual stocks are not just a training ground. They are a way to create liquidity, earn dividends, and capitalize on trends before the crowd catches on. A few outstanding holdings can alter your entire financial trajectory if you stay patient and disciplined.

Then comes 5% in a high-yield savings account, your emergency cash reserve. This is your buffer for emergencies, such as a job loss, unexpected bills, or a sudden income gap. Your cash should earn a rate that tracks short-term interest rates, not 0.01% sitting idle at a legacy bank. Keep it accessible, keep it earning.

Crypto takes 5%, your upside innovation bet. Prioritize proven networks like Bitcoin for store of value and Ethereum for infrastructure. It is asymmetric exposure, enough to matter if it works, small enough not to hurt if it does not.

Your business buying allocation sits around 10%. This is the move from owning paper assets to owning direct cash flow. The right five-figure acquisition, operated long enough, can realistically produce millions over a career.

The Progress Path

This is the structure that connects money to motion. It has three parts: a defined endpoint, an asset allocator, and a series of checkpoints that show how the portfolio builds over time.

The endpoint is $2.5M in diversified liquid investments.

The allocator provides structure, preventing emotional decisions and assigning each dollar a role. Instead of guessing where to invest next, you already know the target mix and can rebalance with discipline. The portfolio design builds balance by default. It spreads risk, limits exposure, and keeps growth aligned with your income and asset goals.

The checkpoints help you stay oriented. They define your current phase, clarify the next target, and ensure you complete each stage before advancing. This approach makes progress both measurable and intentional.

First Quarter: Your goal is to put the structure in place. Push earned income to six figures and automate investment flow. From that $120,000 income, direct capital into your $55,000 portfolio: $22,000 in ETFs, $11,000 in money markets, $11,000 in individual stocks, $2,750 in high-yield savings, $2,750 in crypto, and $5,500 toward a business or future acquisition. The early years focus on setting up the structure, not generating returns. Open every account, link automations, and get to know how each vehicle operates. By the end of Year 2, you have a structure and a small but mighty income working in your favor.

Second Quarter: Your capital base is now established and growing. Earned income rises to around $150,000 a year. Portfolio value reaches $250,000. ETFs make up $100,000 of that base, with $50,000 in money markets and $50,000 in individual stocks. High-yield savings and crypto sit at $12,500 each, and your business buying fund grows to $25,000.

	Q1	Q2	Q3	Q4
EARNED INCOME	$120,000	$150,000	$250,000	$400,000
ETFS (40%)	$22,000	$100,000	$400,000	$1,000,000
MONEY MARKETS (20%)	$11,000	$50,000	$200,000	$500,000
INDIVIDUAL STOCKS (20%)	$11,000	$50,000	$200,000	$500,000
HIGH-YIELD SAVINGS (5%)	$2,750	$12,500	$50,000	$125,000
CRYPTO (5%)	$2,750	$12,500	$50,000	$125,000
BUSINESSES (10%)	$5,500	$25,000	$100,000	$250,000
TOTAL PORTFOLIO	$55,000	$250,000	$1,000,000	$2,500,000

The Pure Progress Portfolio

Third Quarter: Earned income exceeds $250,000. Portfolio value breaks $1M with $400,000 in ETFs, $200,000 each in money markets and individual stocks. You also have $50,000 each in high-yield savings and crypto. Business acquisition capital grows to $100,000.

Fourth Quarter: Earned income moves past $400,000. The portfolio approaches $2.5M, with roughly $1M in ETFs and $1M across stocks and money markets. The remaining allocation includes $125,000 in both high-yield savings and crypto, with $250,000 set aside for business buying.

This is pure investing architecture. Earned income feeds the portfolio, and measured allocations over time create diversification across liquid assets.

Owning the Market

An index is a scoreboard for a group of assets. The S&P 500 tracks the 500 biggest United States companies. The NASDAQ tracks the tech-driven heartbeat of the United States economy. The FTSE 100 mirrors Britain's giants, and the Nikkei 225 captures Japan's corporate elite. Each index tells a story about a market's health and direction.

Index funds allow you to own the entire market story, rather than guessing which chapter will succeed. They copy the index, hold every company inside it, and move with the market itself. That means instant diversification, minimal fees, and no manager guessing with your money. In 1993, the first Exchange-Traded Fund hit the market: the SPDR S&P 500 Trust, SPY. It was designed to track the S&P 500 and make diversified investing accessible to anyone. It exploded for a reason: one trade, hundreds of companies, minimal cost.

Tactical Tip: Automate a $1,000 monthly investment of SPY into your liquid brokerage account.

Inside an ETF might be companies, government bonds, or even gold. You can hold United States Treasuries through SHY or own gold through GLD. ETFs are the modern investor's Swiss Army knife: low cost, easy to buy and sell, and unlimited variety.

Once you understand how to own the market, the question stops being what to buy and becomes how much and how often.

Simple Growth Play

Warren Buffett has long called index fund ETFs the best asset for everyday investors—and he's right.

From 1971 to 2021, the S&P 500 has averaged roughly 7% to 10% annually with dividends reinvested. Some years surge higher, others fall sharply. Over time, investors who stay in the market tend to win.

Investing $1,000 per month into SPDR S&P 500 ETF Trust (SPY) for 25 years adds up to about $300,000 contributed. Historically, that consistent habit has grown to more than $1M. Roughly $700,000 of that comes from market gains—not extra effort.[16]

Here's the move. Open a brokerage account. Set up automated buys of SPY, the ETF that tracks the S&P 500. Hold it. Add consistently.[17]

If you invest about $1.4M into SPY and the market delivers its historical average return, you'll earn roughly $100,000 a year in growth and dividends.

This is a proven, almost boring wealth-building strategy. The hard part isn't the investing. It's earning enough surplus income to fund it consistently. Once you see that this path can make you a liquid millionaire, finding the money gets easier.

Income Through Assets

Dividends and bond payouts are the investor's rent checks. Companies and governments pay you for holding their assets. It is money earned by ownership rather than effort. Every dollar you invest is like an employee working for you.

Dividend ETFs hold companies that regularly pay cash to shareholders. Your dividend yield is simply the annual cash you receive divided by what you invested. Over time, those payments create a steady income stream that feels more predictable than a paycheck.

Bond ETFs work the same way, only through interest instead of profit. By holding hundreds of bonds, they pass on the interest payments to investors, often on a monthly basis. The result is a constant flow of cash that appears whether markets rise or fall. It is the unwavering heartbeat of a portfolio that values reliability as much as return.

ETF	Description	Investment Amount	Yield
VWOB	Emerging market government bonds	$500,000	$27,900
VYMI	Global high-dividend stocks	$500,000	$22,250
VCLT	Long-term corporate bonds	$500,000	$24,100
BNDX	International bonds	$500,000	$22,750
Total	-	**$2,000,000**	**$97,000**

ETF Income Portfolio

Combining dividend and bond ETFs creates a balance between growth and consistency. Dividend stocks offer upside potential when markets climb, while bonds protect your income when volatility hits.

When the income hits your account, you face a choice. You can reinvest it to expand your holdings, use the cash to buy other assets, or take it as investment income.

This portfolio design produces income at scale with minimal risk. With $2M invested across balanced dividend and bond ETFs, you can expect roughly $100,000 a year in income.

This portfolio isn't about maximizing upside. It's for Operators who value reliable cash flow today over uncertain growth tomorrow.

Your Savings Base

Your savings account is not a waiting room; it's a key account in your financial plan. The money stored there safeguards your peace of mind and ensures instant access when things happen. Traditional banks offer minimal returns, but newer institutions and online platforms often provide yields of several percentage points. Savings exist to buy time. That means holding $50,000 to $100,000 in cash so no short-term surprise forces bad decisions. Treat your savings like a strategic asset, not spare change. Do not let banks profit off your deposits while paying you nothing. They are earning a return on your money, so should you.

Cash Yield Vehicles

You buy these money market funds much like an individual stock. They take your capital and invest it in short-term, low-risk debt issued by governments and financial institutions, paying you a steady yield with minimal volatility. Think of them as the calm middle ground between checking accounts and long-term investments—steady, accessible, and reliable.

Many top-tier options, such as Vanguard Federal Money Market Fund (VMFXX), Fidelity Government Money Market Fund (SPAXX), and Schwab Value Advantage Money Fund

(SWVXX), typically deliver around 4% to 5% annual yield, often with a minimum investment around $3,000.[18]

These funds offer highly stable returns, help offset inflation, and serve as an effective high-yield holding place for your cash.

Equity Selection

Once your ETFs, cash reserves, and money markets are in place, individual equities provide upside. This is not speculation. This allocation represents roughly 20% of your portfolio.

These positions are intentionally concentrated. Five to ten companies at most. Real ownership means concentrated positions, not a scattered list of small bets. The goal is not to recreate an index. If you want index behavior, buy the index.

Every position requires a thesis. You should know why the business can outperform over the next several years and what would break that thesis.

This bucket is for proven winners. Category leaders with scale, pricing power, and earnings. You are not making speculative bets on the unknown. You are buying quality and letting execution do the work.

Risk is higher here, but so is impact. One great business, held through cycles, can materially change your portfolio value. That only works if positions are sized deliberately and held through volatility.

A small group of exceptional businesses across different industries is enough.

This bucket rewards judgment and long-term ownership. You are buying pieces of companies you expect to still matter a decade from now.

Core Crypto Stack

Crypto is marketed as the future of money, culture, and finance. The upside is real, but so is the downside. The disciplined way to participate is through the Crypto Trio: three assets, defined exposure.

Bitcoin is the foundation. It is digital gold: scarce, valuable, and globally adopted. Institutions hold it, ETFs now include it, and it has survived every crash and obituary. If you own only one crypto asset, make it this.

Ethereum sits in the middle. It powers stablecoins, decentralized finance, and tokenized assets. Staked Ethereum earns yield while you hold. It is not a trend. It is infrastructure, and traditional finance knows it.

At the top is Solana. The asymmetric bet. Faster, cheaper, riskier. It is where innovation and volatility meet. You do not build your nest egg on it, but a small position can create outsized returns if adoption continues.

This is your crypto core, capture it to cash in on this new asset class. No meme coins.

Buy the Business You Know

Most investors spend decades watching other people's companies grow. Operators take a different path. They buy in.

Nearly 70% of self-made millionaires built their wealth through business ownership—not stock picking or property flipping.[19]

They didn't reinvent the wheel; they found something that worked and made it work harder.

This is not about laundromats or vending machines. Operators buy asset-light businesses that run where they already operate: online, remote, and connected to their existing expertise. A B2B software tool with recurring revenue. A consulting firm in your niche. A content business selling to buyers you already know. The acquisition extends your unique skill set. You are not starting over but buying a shortcut into a market you understand.

Matt acquired a near-dead digital product platform when the previous owner had run out of runway. Most product businesses require years of development, testing, and pre-launch effort before seeing a dollar. Matt relaunched it in three months. Within ninety days, it was generating $10,000 a month.

Target profitable, proven businesses inside your lane. Tech, professional services, digital products. Study the deals, read the financials, lead the people. This is active ownership, not passive income.

Experience is your edge. Buy the business where that edge matters most.

The $2M Ownership Play

Business ownership is the capstone of *Predictable Income*. It's not a 40-year stream like employment or freelancing. It happens in five-year tours of duty built around one repeatable process: buy, build, scale, and operate.

Over a 40-year career, you complete four buy-and-build cycles. Each tour generates about $100,000 in annual profit, producing $500,000 in lifetime value over five years. Run that play four times, and you create $2M in total earnings.

You are not chasing exits or lottery wins. You are building a monthly cash flow. Own businesses that throw off profit. Target companies where you can pay yourself a respectable salary as the owner.

At this stage, you're ready for entrepreneurship at the highest level. These businesses add significant chunks to your net worth and allow you to complete the $2.5M final mission portfolio.

Turning Investments into Income

You put $5,000 a year into a broad market ETF like SPY or VTI and let it grow. The market averages around a 7% annual return. After five years, your initial contributions of $25,000 have grown to approximately $30,000 in your liquid taxable brokerage account.

Now it is time to flip from building to harvesting. You withdraw 4% a year, around $1,000. That $1,000 moves straight into your personal checking account. It is income now, paid from your investments rather than your labor. The remaining balance keeps growing.

Never take out more than your portfolio can replace. If your assets grow around 7% a year and you withdraw 4%, you are still in the green. The base grows while you're being paid. That is how invested capital becomes a permanent paycheck.

Choosing Your Style

Each investor runs their playbook differently. Some want to touch every lever and stay hands-on. Others wish to invest on autopilot. The question is not which style is better, but which one fits the bandwidth you actually have. Many of us underestimate how much time and attention active investing requires.

If you are already managing a full-time job, freelancing, or running a business, your schedule is at capacity. Adding active trading, stock picking, or portfolio rebalancing becomes another job entirely. This is where most Operators benefit from a passive approach. Set up automatic investments into low-cost ETFs and let them run. Your attention belongs on increasing income, not watching markets.

Passive investing is a way to grow your money with minimal effort and attention. You invest automatically, protect your time, and let your returns compound. Many investors fail not because of poor returns, but because they get distracted or make emotional decisions during market fluctuations. Stick with it. Stay fully invested and keep contributing capital.

Active investors treat investing like a business and spend real time researching, analyzing, and managing positions. This requires strong processes, emotional restraint, and the ability to separate signal from noise. When done correctly, it can outperform, but it also consumes the most limited resource of all: time. Without a frame, active investing easily becomes speculation disguised as work.

Your investment style should match your current operating load. If your income flywheel is already running fast, the smart move is to automate and maintain ease. Passive investing gives you leverage through time. If you have the structure and bandwidth for active investing, treat it as a separate enterprise with its own goals, capital, and accountability.

Build your investing plan the same way you build your income system by matching resources to real constraints. Whether you use automation or hands-on analysis, the objective is the same: consistent, aggressive investing in high-quality, high-growth, liquid assets.

Entry and Exit Rules

Enter small. Start with a toe in the water, not a cannonball. Invest $100 into an ETF. Each move is reconnaissance, testing how capital behaves in the market.

Expand when the signal is clear. Once familiar with the terrain and risk, scale up. Double your buys, automate them. Allocate more to what is working.

Regulate your exit plans. Most investors panic. You trim winners and cut losers. Unwind in slices, never all at once. Exiting is not retreat. It is reallocation, preparing for the next offensive.

Use dollar-cost averaging to automate entry and exit, adding consistently when markets fall and taking profits gradually when targets are hit.

Modern Portfolio Tools

Technology has made advanced investing accessible to anyone with a bank account. A robo-advisor applies the same principles you've learned—and runs them automatically. Think of a robo-advisor as a blend of a financial advisor and artificial intelligence.[20]

You link your bank account, choose your risk level, and the platform handles the investing and rebalancing for you.

It's not magic. It's code. It allocates across equities and bonds, reinvests dividends, and adjusts as conditions change. Fees stay low, behavior remains consistent, and returns follow.

You still own the strategy. The automation handles the repetition. That partnership is what Operator investing should be. You can focus on earning more and living better, while your robo-advisor manages the day-to-day of your portfolio.

Staying Liquid

Liquidity is not just a portfolio metric. It is a life strategy. On the investment side, liquidity means owning assets you can convert to cash without penalty, delay, or a phone call to a broker. Stocks, ETFs, and money market funds qualify. Real estate, private equity, and most business holdings do not. That distinction matters more than most investors realize. When opportunity appears or crisis hits, the people who move fastest are rarely the smartest. They are the most liquid.

Matt learned this during the pandemic. While others were locked into physical businesses, long-term leases, and illiquid assets, he was running a consulting business from a laptop in Los Angeles. When a new opportunity surfaced in San Diego, he went for it without anchors. No warehouse to sublease. No equipment to sell. No staff to relocate. He moved in three weeks.

On the lifestyle side, liquidity means the same thing. Avoid accumulating assets that own you back. Multiple properties, luxury vehicles, and physical businesses create obligations that follow you everywhere. They limit your ability to relocate for a better role, take a sabbatical, or pivot when the market shifts.

The goal is not minimalism. It is optionality. Own things that give you choices rather than remove them. Keep your balance sheet light enough that your next move is always available to you.

Rich Enough

Most people spend their career trading time for money. Investing reverses that equation. Every dollar you place into the market is a unit of time you will never have to sell again. The goal is to get rich enough. Rich enough that your portfolio funds your life on your terms. That is what the $2.5M portfolio target is really about. Not a number on a screen. A $100,000 annual withdrawal that funds your life. That crossover is the real finish line.

CHAPTER 6: DOLLAR DEFENSE

"It's not how much money you make but how much money you keep, how hard it works for you, and how many generations you keep it for."

— Robert Kiyosaki

You built the engines. Now don't let them burn down. Most operators lose money the same way they earn it: fast, confident, and without seeing it coming.

After years of false starts, Matt finally broke through. He had founded an e-commerce platform and in year one it crossed $1M in sales. Revenue was climbing fast. The dashboards were green. He felt close to real scale.

Then he accelerated. He hired a CTO. Built a new app. Added contractors. Subscribed to better tools. Fixed costs rose quickly. Revenue kept growing, but margins stayed thin. Cash flow turned tight. Instead of stabilizing operations, he borrowed to maintain speed. A $100,000 partner loan. Another $100,000 in advances from Stripe and PayPal. When revenue dipped for a few months, credit cards bridged the gap.

He wasn't scaling anymore. He was financing fragility. Within a year, debt obligations exceeded operating cash flow. The business couldn't service its loans and fund growth at the same time. He shut it down and walked away with $50,000 in business credit card debt.

That is the debt spiral. It doesn't announce itself. It starts with one reasonable decision, then another, until the weight of obligation outpaces the possibility of recovery.

None of it means anything if the defensive layer fails. Not the job, not the freelance engine, not the investments. Income without protection is just a longer fall.

The lesson is not to fear debt but to respect it. Borrowing magnifies whatever already exists, whether order or disorder. Use it to expand what is proven, not to rescue what is uncertain.

Stability before speed. Protect cash flow like oxygen.

The Hidden Second Game

Earning money is the first act. Most people never make it to the second.

They chase raises, bonuses, side hustles. Then watch the gains leak out through lifestyle creep, bad debt, and careless spending. The income grows, but wealth doesn't and they wonder why.

Forget the blanket rules you have been fed: "Debt is bad," "Cut every expense," "Save your way to success." That is financial kindergarten. Some debt is an accelerator. Some spending is an investment. The goal is not to spend less. It is to spend with intention, stripping away waste while keeping the things that actually move your life and income forward.

Think of it as two games running at the same time. The offensive game is building income. The defensive game is protecting what you build. Most professionals are playing offense while ignoring defense entirely. Operators play both.

Tactical Tip: Set every credit card to autopay the minimum to avoid late fees, then attack the principal aggressively.

The first defensive move is: know your burn rate.

Your burn rate is the total amount of money you spend each month across your personal life and your businesses combined. Track it like a business metric. When you know the number, you gain power over it. Operators can quote their monthly numbers on demand. If you cannot, that is where to start.

The Tax Gradient

Taxes are your largest expense. The average earner treats taxes like the weather, inevitable and uncontrollable. Operators treat them like a cost line they can manage.

Every country runs its own code, but the pattern is universal. In California, a $300,000 income might drop to $180,000 after taxes. In London, Toronto, or Sydney, it's the same curve wearing a different flag. Taxes are unavoidable, and the government always takes its share first.

Amateurs and earners differ not in income, but in strategy. In a passive tax position, income is taxed first, and you keep what's left. In an active tax position, you control how and when income is taxed.

You don't have to flee to Dubai to run this play. You just have to change categories. Employees get taxed on income. Entrepreneurs get taxed on profit. The more you control how money flows to you, the more you get to decide how much you keep. Freelance income is raw and dangerous. It feels like freedom until the tax bill shows up. This income runs through your business account, covers expenses, and whatever's left is profit. That profit and your salary are what the tax authority cares about. Each client payment that lands, you move 30% to 35% into a separate tax account. Not checking, never business, but a brokerage account portfolio for taxes. Park it in a money market or short-term Treasury fund earning meaningful interest. Your tax cash now works instead of dying in a zero-interest account.

Then use your business expenses as your weapon. Invest in tools, education, and other legitimate business expenses before the tax year ends. You aren't dodging taxes but directing them. You structure your own tax liability rather than just taking whatever Uncle Sam has in store for you.

The rich don't hate taxes. They understand them. They operate from an advantageous position, flatten the gradient, and design their income to maximize deductions and expenses.

The Big 3

The typical professional chases pennies while ignoring dollars. They bring brown-bag lunches, clip coupons, and still feel broke because the real leaks run through three channels: housing, transportation, and food. These are the Big 3. Control the Big 3 and the defensive layer almost takes care of itself.

Housing eats the largest share of income. The danger lies in mistaking wants for needs: a bigger house in the right neighborhood, a spare room that never gets used, a mortgage stretched to the limit. Smaller homes, smarter locations, flexible living arrangements. That is where the savings actually live.

Next comes transportation, the most seductive wealth killer on the list. Payments, insurance, gas, repairs, and depreciation add up fast. A luxury car might feel like a reward, but it's usually a financial disaster waiting to happen. Walk when you can. Share when you can. If you must buy, choose a used, fuel-efficient car that fits your life, not your image.

The third drain is food. Delivery apps, takeout, and grocery splurges blur together until the damage is done. The fix is not starvation. It is thoughtfulness. Cook more often. Plan your meals. Buy in bulk.

Stop bragging about canceling Netflix. The significant cuts come from housing, transportation, and food. That's the fat you trim to feed your future.

The Cost Curve

There are two lines in debt management: the Growth Line and the Cost Line. One measures how fast your income and investments compound. The other tracks how fast your debt works against you.

Your mission is to ensure the Growth Line stays above the Cost Line. Always. When your money grows faster than your debt, you have the advantage. When debt grows faster than your money, you are on borrowed time.

Debt is a rate game. What you owe has a cost. What you own has a return. The spread between them tells you everything. If you borrow at 5% and earn 10%, that difference grows rapidly in your favor. But if you borrow at 20% and earn 8%, your money shrinks quickly. Every dollar you make gets eaten by interest before it can grow.

The Cost Curve shows who is really winning. The bank or you? When your Growth Line rises steeper than your Cost Line, you are expanding your margin. That margin is what lets you take risks, move fast, and sleep at night.

If the lines ever cross, everything flips. You cannot outwork compounding interest once it is working against you.

Maintain a growth rate higher than your cost rate. Grow income faster. Grow investments faster. Borrow only when the return beats the rate.

This is how you measure financial control. By the spread of what you earn and what you owe. Operators keep that spread positive and growing. When your Growth Line outruns your Cost Line, you are no longer surviving debt. You are mastering it.

The Interest Equation

Debt is not a villain. It's a variable. Every form of borrowing carries a cost, and those numbers tell you exactly which debts build you and which bleed you.

The cheapest money is housing debt. A mortgage usually has an interest rate between 2% to 8%. That's ownership debt. You're borrowing against a tangible asset, one that holds or grows value over time. When the payment fits your income and the property serves your life, that kind of debt can move you forward.

Next come business loans and student loans. They tend to live from 5% to 12% interest. This is the leverage zone. If the loan funds something that increases your earning power, like a new product, a proven business, or a degree that raises your income, it can accelerate progress. Borrowing at 10% to earn 30% is smart leverage. But that same 10% loan used to chase an unproven idea or a vague plan turns into a weight.

DEBT TYPE	INTEREST RATE	PURPOSE	OUTCOME
Business Loan	5–12%	Growth Capital	Builds Income
Mortgage	2–8%	Asset Ownership	Builds Stability
Student Loan	3–9%	Skill Acquisition	Expands Earning Power
Auto Loan	6–10%	Lifestyle Convenience	Shrinks Cash Flow
Credit Card / BNPL	15–30%	Consumption	Limits Growth

The Interest Equation

Then there's transportation. Car loans typically fall in the 6% to 10% range. They seem harmless, but most of that money funds depreciation. You're paying interest on something that loses 15% of its worth the moment you drive it off the lot. A 7% loan on a car that loses $20,000 in value in three years is a losing trade.

Mission Brief: Keep non-mortgage debt under 25% of your annual income and cycle it back to zero as fast as possible.

At the bottom of the spectrum sits consumer debt. Credit cards, store financing, and buy now, pay later plans range from 15% to 30% interest. That is the kill zone. A credit card with a 20%

interest rate doubles your balance in just over three years if you only make minimum payments. A buy-now-pay-later plan charging 25% turns a $1,000 purchase into a $1,500 expense.

Low-interest debt builds capacity. Mid-interest debt can accelerate growth when managed carefully. High-interest debt destroys it all.

Operators know precisely what every borrowed dollar costs and what it earns in return.

The Pay Down Protocol

Paying off debt is not about perfection. It is about momentum. The play that works is the one you can run every month without burning out. Here are ten approaches that work.

1. *Start Small*: Pay off your smallest balance first. The win is real and the momentum is real. Once it is gone, move to the next one.
2. *Chase the Rate*: Switch to the highest interest balance once you have early momentum. This is where the math works in your favor.
3. *Consolidate Yourself*: Juggling five due dates? Roll them into one lower-rate account. Fewer moving parts mean fewer mistakes. Do not rebuild debt on the old lines.
4. *Transfer the Balance*: Move high-interest debt to a 0% promotional card and attack it before the window closes. One rule: the old card goes in a drawer.
5. *Pick a Percentage*: Choose 10%, 15%, or 20% of income and treat it like rent. Non-negotiable. Automated payments equal automated discipline.

6. *Deploy Windfalls*: Bonus, tax refund, side income. All of it goes to the principal. No exceptions.
7. *Protect the Essentials*: Mortgage and car before credit cards. Lose those and the damage spreads fast.
8. *Use Technology*: Debt tracking apps turn a grind into a scoreboard. Find one and use it.
9. *Pause Retirement Temporarily*: Drowning in 20%+ interest? Consider pausing contributions briefly and redirecting everything at the debt. Restart the moment it clears.
10. *Do a 30-Day Freeze*: One month. No discretionary spending. Every dollar that does not leave your account accelerates the payoff. Most people are surprised how little they actually miss.

Debt does not disappear on its own. Pick a play, run it every month, and keep going until the number hits zero.

The Total Collapse

Bankruptcy rarely begins with a catastrophe. It begins with confidence and a string of reasonable decisions that slowly become a crisis.

Aaron dropped out of Stanford Business School in 1999 to found LeaseExchange, an internet company he believed in enough to raise $5M for. By 2001, it was bankrupt. Not because the idea was wrong. Because revenue never materialized. He had hired a VP of sales and assumed the problem was solved. It wasn't. By the time he understood what was missing, the runway was gone. The lessons were hard: know how to sell before you hire someone to do it. Run the leanest team possible until revenue is proven.

Be ruthless about costs. Scaling before the engine works does not accelerate growth. It accelerates collapse.

The five most common causes of personal bankruptcy are medical bills, job loss, poor money management, personal emergencies, and high-interest debt. Medical expenses alone account for 62% of personal bankruptcies in the United States.[21] One diagnosis, one hospital stay, one gap in coverage—and the floor disappears.

The defense is not complicated. Lock in health coverage before you need it. Eliminate high-interest debt before it builds. Have liquid cash on hand for your emergency fund before the emergency arrives. Grow additional income sources before the primary one stalls.

None of this is reactive. All of it is built in advance.

You don't wake up bankrupt. You get there one drip, one decision, and one delay at a time.

Operational Discipline

In a perfect world, you would run debt-free and lean. No balances. No lenders. No drag. In the real world, we use tools, and debt is one of them. It is powerful, dangerous, and easy to misuse.

Compounding builds wealth when you invest and destroys it when you borrow. Every dollar of debt is someone else's asset. You are their yield. The bank, the credit card company, and the lender are the house. They always play to win.

Operational discipline means knowing which side of the table you are on, whether you're the lender or the borrower.

Think of spending like investing. Each purchase is a bet on your future. Spend on good assets: healthy food, reasonable housing, inexpensive transport. Avoid bad investments beyond these. Every dollar you waste is capital that could have provided a return.

Discipline is defense. You protect your downside so you can swing bigger on the upside. Do not avoid risk. Manage it. Know which moves carry the highest risk, and only take the ones you understand.

Play small on debt, strategic with expenses, and big on growth.

CHAPTER 7: BLIND SPOTS

"Success is a stack of choices. Not one big moment, but a steady pile of gritty, deliberate decisions to keep showing up. You're not behind. You're building."

— Dr. Bhrett McCabe

Most money books skip this part. They show you the charts and the potential upside. They talk about economic security. They gloss over the days when nothing works, the months when you feel stuck, and the years when progress feels slower than you expected.

This plan is ambitious: three income lines, a $300,000 annual income target, and a $10M career. A $2.5M portfolio that can pay you $100,000 a year at a 4% withdrawal rate.

All of that is possible. None of it is guaranteed.

Many readers assume there is a clean version of this process. A version where the job change lands on schedule, freelancing clicks quickly, investing rises steadily, and confidence follows.

That version does not exist. Real progress is uneven. One income source moves while another stalls. You understand the system long before you can run it smoothly. Some weeks feel aligned. Other stretches feel slow.

Your finances will never mirror the diagrams. The system is a map, not a mirror. Friction does not mean something is broken. Confusion does not mean you lack ability. Early effort feels inefficient because you are building expertise, not just outcomes.

This work happens alongside a full life. Jobs, relationships, and obligations keep moving while you build in parallel. Disorder is part of the deal.

Expect gaps. Expect uneven effort. Expect to do things out of sequence.

Progress comes from staying engaged through imperfect execution. You adjust when reality pushes back. You simplify when capacity is limited. You press when timing allows.

Action comes before readiness. This is what real-world building looks like. Not clean. Not linear. Still effective over time.

Who doesn't like a big plan on day one? The idea of making more, investing more, and building something of your own feels exciting.

Then the first freelance client takes more time than expected. The first serious job search drags past month three. The market dips right after you finally start investing.

It is easy to assume this means the plan is broken. That you are doing it wrong. That you are not cut out for this.

You're still in the early stages: the boring part where you plant seeds and stare at dirt.

There's nothing supernatural about *Predictable Income*. It's repetition stacked over time. When you feel the urge to tap out, you're usually inches from victory.

Companies care about their agenda, not yours. The moment you build competencies or income outside the job, they take note even if they act like they don't. Don't look for applause for weekend freelancing or smarter investing. Don't expect support for anything that raises your value beyond their walls.

Do your job well, stay sharp, and understand that financial freedom is your win, not theirs.

Side income seems straightforward from the outside. Create a service, send a few emails, collect checks. That is the fantasy.

Reality looks different. Messages go unanswered. You hear a hundred no's for every yes. You underprice at first, overpromise on a project, and finish great work only to chase the invoice.

Push through the wrong way, and you get stressed, bitter, and burnt out. Worse, you drag that frustration back into your main job and damage both.

But if you stick with it, you evolve. You prove to yourself that you can create value outside a paycheck. You stop thinking like an employee. That identity is worth more than any single invoice, and you only earn it by getting through the rough beginning.

Investing Volatility

On paper, investing looks like a smooth curve. Your money grows at 7% a year, and everyone chills. But in markets, the line jumps around. One year, you are up 15%. The following year, you are down 20%. Headlines scream. Friends panic.

You will feel an urge to stop contributing just when you should keep going. You will feel tempted to pull money out right after prices fall instead of giving them time to recover. You will see others brag about fast wins in high-stakes bets and feel like you are behind.

The danger is not just losing money. It's losing your nerve and breaking your own plan.

Stay in the market. Keep allocating capital to your investments.

Three income sources sound aggressive. It can quickly turn into "work all the time" if you are not careful.

If you say yes to every task, every client, every opportunity, you will eventually hit a wall. When that happens, you do not just lose your side income. You lose your drive in your main job, your patience with the people you care about, and your ability to think clearly.

Predictable Income is built for the long haul. It is a career system, not a quick cash play. One strategic tour of duty at a time. One clear freelance offer. A single, enduring investment strategy.

You cannot maintain 12 new habits, three new jobs, and see to your personal life at the same time. You will need seasons of rest, focused weeks, and honest conversations with yourself about what you can realistically carry.

Ignoring your limits can lead to losing everything you've worked to build.

Different Starting Lines

Some of us have six months of savings, supportive partners, and friends in high places. Others are managing major debts, caring for family members, and starting with a low salary and no network.

These paths are not equal. We should not pretend they are.

If you start from a more challenging position, your pace may be slower. You might need to address debt first or focus on building one income stream before expanding to others. Your first freelance client may pay less. Your first investment contributions may be small.

This doesn't mean you're out of the running. It simply means you'll need more time, patience, and an extended runway to reach your goal.

At some point, you'll lose a job, a client, money in the market, or even your motivation. There will be mornings when you do not want to send another outreach message. Evenings when looking at your budget sounds like hell. On nights when fear and shame whisper that you're not a true Operator, it can feel like your only option is to throw in the towel.

This is normal and part of the process. An Operator stays locked in. You stack cash so a rough patch doesn't rattle you. You keep relationships alive so you're never starting cold. You train your craft so opportunity doesn't catch you flat-footed. You bargain hard when you join a team and just as hard when you leave one. You plan for the ugly quarter while the current one is still printing green.

The biggest pitfall is believing you are the exception who will never get knocked down.

If this chapter has one purpose, it is to remove illusions. This plan will test your patience. It will demand clear thinking when you are tired. It will ask you to say no to things that feel good in the moment so you can say yes to better things later.

If that sounds painful, it is. But you know what is worse? Waking up at 60 with one shaky income source, no savings, and no options. You're not here for an easy path; you're here for one that works. No ambitious undertaking is without risk, and *Predictable Income* is no different. This process will be volatile.

You do not need perfect conditions. You need clear eyes and determination.

If you accept these realities up front, the hard days will not surprise you. You will still feel them. You just will not mistake them for the end of the road. You chose this path with the lights on. This is how adults build wealth.

CHAPTER 8: TIME IN COCKPIT

"I'm convinced that about half of what separates the successful entrepreneurs from the non-successful ones is pure perseverance."

— Steve Jobs

When we started writing this book, the direction seemed obvious. It wasn't.

The first title was *$300K Parlay*. It captured ambition but not the full architecture. Then we shifted to *Income Operating System*. That felt structured and technical. For a while, it seemed right. But as the manuscript expanded, something kept bothering us. The title described the machinery, not the outcome readers actually cared about.

So we kept rewriting. More feedback. More changes.

Three years in, the answer surfaced. *Predictable Income*. The name expressed the result. It paired naturally with Aaron's book, *Predictable Revenue*. Now, it feels like it was always the only option.

It took three years to find two words.

That is time in cockpit.

Airline pilots don't handle turbulence because they read about aviation. They handle it because they've logged thousands of hours across hundreds of flights. They've seen warning lights flash. They've flown through storms. They've diverted, delayed, and landed in conditions that would unnerve anyone without the reps. After enough cycles, volatility stops feeling random. It becomes something you've seen before and know how to move through.

Careers work the same way.

That entire process is an example of the Heat Lock Loop. A heat-seeking missile does not start with precision. It begins with wide movements, gathers signal, and tightens its path only after enough adjustments. Early attempts feel inefficient because you're still collecting the information you need. Once enough cycles accumulate, decisions that were once blurry become sharp.

Careers develop the same way. Judgment improves as you work through different roles, clients, incentives, and environments. Early moves involve more guesswork. Later moves benefit from accumulated context. We start to see which opportunities hold up under scrutiny and which were never solid to begin with.

Predictable Cycles

A working life becomes far easier to manage once you see it as a set of defined chapters instead of an undefined stretch of years. Operators rely on this structure. Across a full career, an Operator completes around 13 employment runs, works with roughly

200 freelance clients, and acquires about 4 businesses. That is 217 total cycles. Once you see the limits, you know what you are building toward.

Start with employment. You will only complete 13 job transitions across your working life. Each averages around three years and produces about $300,000 of earnings, roughly $100,000 per year. Many professionals dislike job hunts because they feel uncomfortable and uncertain. Operators approach them differently. The count is finite. You only need to execute this transition 13 times. Each one is a three-year climb where you advance compensation, increase capability, and position yourself for the next tour. Employment becomes a ladder with 13 steps instead of an endless series of roles.

Stream	# of Cycles	Target Earnings	Earnings Per Cycle
Employment	13	$4,000,000	$307,692
Freelancing	200	$4,000,000	$20,000
Investments (Buy a Business)	4	$2,000,000	$500,000
Total	217	$10,000,000	–

Predictable Cycles Table

The freelance stream brings a wider scale. There are 200 freelance customers, each averaging about $20,000 in income. 200 wins reveal how the freelance engine actually works. It is not built on a handful of perfect clients showing up at the right time. It's built on a foundation of repeatable acquisition. Once you see the volume required, the nature of the work changes. You need a process that can bring in clients at a consistent pace year after year. Positioning, outreach, scoping, pricing, and delivery all depend on your ability to support this level of throughput. With the 200-customer target in front of you, your approach evolves. You stop chasing that one ideal client and start building a sales system capable of generating ongoing demand.

The investment stream comes down to four business acquisitions across a lifetime. The first should be smaller and manageable. The fourth can be larger because experience scales with each buy-then-build process. The guiding principle is straightforward: focus on businesses that produce income from day one. Monthly cash flow covers early mistakes, supports debt service, and gives the acquisition breathing room. Sourcing these opportunities requires extensive filtering. Operators may review hundreds of businesses to find one worth pursuing. This search is part of the process itself. Through repetition, you develop judgment around margins, customer concentration, owner dependence, pricing power, and durability of revenue. By the fourth acquisition, your decisions are far more disciplined.

When you line all three streams together, the architecture stands out. 13 employment runs. 200 freelance engagements. 4 acquisitions. These are the defined Operator missions. They give structure, pacing, and direction. Once you know the count, you stop bouncing from role to role or project to project. You pick the phase you are in. You define what each evolution must accomplish.

The Operator Lens

Most professionals react to their career. A role stalls, and they update their resume. A client churns, and they spiral. An acquisition falls through, and they question the strategy.

Operators do something different. They locate themselves. When something changes, they ask one question first: which stream is this and what does this phase still need to produce?

The employment run has eight months left and needs $80,000 more. The freelance engine has 60 wins and needs 140 more. The first acquisition is generating cash and the second search has already started.

The event is not the story. The cycle is. When you know the count, you know the plan. Every opportunity, setback, and decision fits somewhere in the structure.

That is what time in the cockpit actually builds. Not just experience. A lens.

CHAPTER 9: OPERATOR MODE

"Don't be a one-trick pony.
Diversify your income streams."

— Suze Orman

Thanksgiving was a few days out. The house finally sat on the same solid footing as the rest of his finances. It wasn't held together by luck, but forged through deliberate decisions. Matt stood by the window and watched the last streaks of daylight move across the pool. Another year behind him. A year of gains, losses, pivots, and progress. For the first time, he wasn't ending the year unsure of where he stood. He knew exactly what he had built.

The year began the way so many tech years begin. A layoff. A manager reading off a script he barely understood. The kind of moment that used to knock Matt back on his heels. The kind of moment that once dictated his future for months.

This time he didn't budge. He knew he had an operating method he could now count on. Three engines. Defined actions. Clear targets. Executable missions.

For generations, we were taught that the safest career path is the one with the fewest disruptions, as though stability alone guarantees security. Operators, however, have a different mindset. They anticipate that a crisis is inevitable and train to absorb the impact, adapt, and continue moving forward.

He walked into the kitchen, poured himself a drink, and reflected on the year. His job carried the base income. His freelance work stood ready with clients and processes. His investments grew without drama.

Early in his career, he believed the answer was effort. Stay later. Push harder. Outwork everyone. But effort alone wasn't enough. The turning point came when he developed a tactical protocol for sequencing moves across defined income lanes, with clear annual and lifetime earnings targets.

That method follows four steps.

First, mindset. You stop acting like a passenger in your own career. You adopt a way of thinking that treats income like an operation. You study risk. You plan your moves. You take responsibility for the direction of your life.

Second, knowledge. You master how to create *Predictable Income*. How employment works. How freelance work creates leverage. How investing builds long-term strength. You learn the accounts, the tools, and the moves.

Third, execution. You build the employment, freelance, and investing engines. You follow the sequence. You run the annual missions.

Fourth, people. The colleagues, partners, mentors, clients, and professionals who raise your standard. Operators never rise alone. They rise because they surround themselves with people who challenge and elevate them.

Mindset. Knowledge. Execution. People. A workable process.

He paused and considered the foundation beneath it all. He had taken the safest income vehicles available today. A solid job. Cash reserves. Broad-market ETFs. Straightforward investing. No gambling. No chasing heat. He built them into a structure with far less exposure than depending on a single manager in a single company.

Critics argue that *Predictable Income* is overly intense or unnecessarily complex, claiming it requires more effort than most people can handle. They think running several engines requires unusual courage and effort. What we have seen is that this OS is the lowest-risk income framework available in the modern economy. And that committed Operators can execute their own version of the system through daily micro-actions.

He walked back to the living room and opened his laptop to study his proven income principles. Annual missions across the three engines. The earning path toward $10M. The transition from earnings to a $2.5M portfolio.

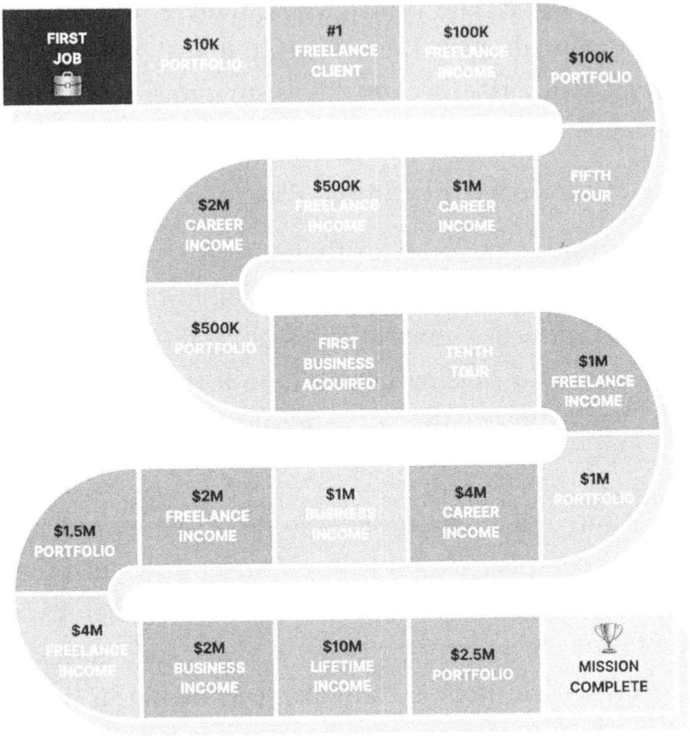

The Operator's Journey

For years, the system lived only in his head. Now it existed outside him. Defined. Structured. Executable.

He thought about the last ten years. The roles he outgrew. The roles that outgrew him. The consulting projects that dragged on. The ones that accelerated his growth. The falls he took. The failures he needed. Each one was practice. Each one shaped him into someone who doesn't fold when conditions change.

Handling risk didn't weaken him; it made him stronger, gave him options, and expanded his reach. It turned his past into training.

That is the Operator identity. Not a job title. Not a mindset trick. A way of living. Constant training. Building skills under pressure. Improving through work, side projects, and smart investments. Operating as someone who expects hard moments and advances anyway.

The next decade would build on the one behind him. More skill. More income. More assets. Mission after mission. Year after year.

He turned off the laptop and walked down the hallway. Thanksgiving was coming. The house would fill soon. Before that, he paused. Not to celebrate. To acknowledge the evolution.

He wasn't driven by fear anymore. He wasn't reacting. He was trained.

He wasn't hoping or guessing. He was prepared.

He had achieved *Predictable Income.*

He was an Operator.

ACKNOWLEDGEMENTS

This book was created with love, an army of beta readers, and backers.

This book would not exist without the help of the contributors below:

Dr. Anthony Smith, Neeraj Pradhan, Nancy Chou, Patrick William Joyce, Zachary Hynek, Alex Felman, Robert Hever, Thomas Allcock, David Keefe, Jimi Olaghere, Justin Michael, Jeremy Jones, James Leonardo, Chris Fedrizzi, Pascal Stieh, Alexis Boucher, Dan San, Marcus Cauchi, Derek Noble, Chris Noble, Zachary Radford, Reg Nordman, Kyle Romaniuk, Joe Natoli, Darius Safavi, Max Carmody, Dom Watson, Guy Wendon, Kalev Kaarna, Henry Williams, Phil Gascoyne, Kornel Tomicki, Michael Tuso, Julian Castelli, Graeme Gilovitz, Caoimhin Gillespie, Pablo Carrillo, Stefan Iacono, Josh Hudson, Daniel Melana, Jacek Gabanowicz, Kiri Nowak, Keith Norris, Florian Rittmeyer, David Ploshay, Betsy Shaak, April Halden, Rahul Kannan, Robert Jacobson, Kristin Campbell, and Carol Olona.

Founding Backers:

- Jon Siegel
- Andre Lavoie
- Pierre Schurmann
- Marde Ross

This book was self-published in the United States. Writing a book takes time, effort, and money to do it right. The following companies financially supported this project, and we are eternally grateful.

- BrandWell (brandwell.ai): Drive traffic from Google and LLMs with optimized content.
- PClub.io (pclub.io): Master sales training and skill formation.
- Process Street (process.st): Improve operational efficiency, quality, and compliance.
- PandaDoc (pandadoc.com): Streamline document workflows and close deals faster.

DISCLAIMER

The content in the *Predictable Income* book, including all digital materials and related resources, is intended solely for educational and informational purposes. The authors and contributors to the *Predictable Income* book are not certified financial advisors; therefore, the economic strategies and advice presented should be viewed as educational content rather than tailored financial counsel.

It is essential to understand that the opinions and analyses expressed in this book are the personal views of the authors and should not be taken as specific investment recommendations. The aim is to enhance your financial literacy and help you make informed decisions, not to prescribe a one-size-fits-all approach to financial management.

The perspectives offered in the *Predictable Income* book are subject to change and are not to be taken as an immutable guide to investing or financial planning. Nothing within this book should be construed as a direct endorsement of any investment strategy or as an encouragement to engage in investment based solely on the content presented. Financial situations are highly individual, and our discussions are meant to inform rather than direct your investment choices.

While we may provide insights into various technological platforms or financial systems, these mentions should not be interpreted as endorsements or recommendations to invest in such platforms.

References to specific securities and their past performance are included for illustrative purposes only and should not be considered as advice to buy or sell those securities. Investment strategies should be carefully considered in light of your personal financial goals, as what may be effective for one individual may not be suitable for another.

Investing always involves risks, including the potential loss of principal. Given the ever-changing nature of financial markets, past performance is not a reliable indicator of future results.

By using the materials in *Predictable Income*, you acknowledge that any advisory services or financial planning guidance will be provided only under formal agreements, where legally permissible and in compliance with all applicable regulations, and that the authors are not licensed financial professionals.

ENDNOTES

Chapter 2: The System

1 U.S. Census Bureau, *Income in the United States*: 2023 (Washington, DC: U.S. Department of Commerce, September 2024), accessed October 15, 2025, https://www2.census.gov/library/publications/2024/demo/p60-282.pdf.

2 Board of Governors of the Federal Reserve System, Survey of Consumer Finances 2022 (Washington, DC: Board of Governors, 2023), accessed October 15, 2025, https://www.federalreserve.gov/econres/scfindex.htm.

3 Gallup, Stock Ownership by Household Income and Age: 2024 Polling Report (Washington, DC: Gallup Organization, May 2024), accessed October 15, 2025, https://news.gallup.com/poll/266807/percentage-americans-owns-stock.aspx.

4 Bureau of Economic Analysis, Personal Saving Rate: National Income and Product Accounts (Washington, DC: U.S. Department of Commerce, 2024), accessed

October 15, 2025, https://www.bea.gov/data/income-saving/personal-saving-rate.

Chapter 3: Employment OS

5 Pew Research Center, Trends in Income and Wealth Inequality (Washington, DC: Pew Research Center, 2020), accessed October 15, 2025, https://www.pewresearch.org/social-trends/2020/01/09/trends-in-income-and-wealth-inequality/.

6 U.S. Bureau of Labor Statistics, Occupational Employment and Wage Statistics (Washington, DC: U.S. Department of Labor, May 2024), accessed October 15, 2025, https://www.bls.gov/oes/methods_24.pdf.

7 Boterview, Average Time to Find a Job by Industry (2026 Statistics), accessed February 8, 2026, https://boterview.com/a/average-time-find-job.

8 Randstad USA, *2024 Severance and Benefits Benchmarking Report* (Atlanta: Randstad, 2024), accessed November 6, 2025, https://www.randstad.com/s3fs-media/rscom/public/2025-02/Randstad_Annual_Report_2024_0.pdf?VersionId=LlTQ.5dhCvH0C3FiBnYOryA5qOtq9aVi

9 The Interview Guys, "Highest Paying Sales Jobs," accessed October 15, 2025, https://blog.theinterviewguys.com/highest-paying-sales-jobs/.

Chapter 4: Freelance OS

10 HubSpot Research, Global Sales Outreach Benchmarks 2024 (Cambridge, MA: HubSpot, 2024), accessed October 15, 2025, https://www.hubspot.com/hubfs/HubSpots%202024%20Sales%20Trends%20Report.pdf.

Chapter 5: Investing OS

11 Forbes Advisor, "Average Stock Market Return," accessed October 2023, https://www.forbes.com/sites/johnjennings/2022/12/31/what-will-the-market-return-in-2023/.

12 U.S. Bureau of Labor Statistics, CPI-U Historical Data (Washington, DC: BLS, 2024), accessed November 6, 2025, https://www.bls.gov/cpi/data.htm

13 Board of Governors of the Federal Reserve System, Distribution of Household Wealth in the U.S. Since 1989 (Washington, DC: Board of Governors, 2024), accessed October 15, 2025, https://www.federalreserve.gov/releases/z1/dataviz/dfa/distribute/table/.

14 Principles for Navigating Big Debt Crises (Westport, CT: Bridgewater Associates, 2018), accessed November 7, 2025, https://www.principles.com/big-debt-crises

15 Morningstar Research Services, Annual Report (Chicago: Morningstar, 2024), accessed November 7, 2025, https://s21.q4cdn.com/198919461/files/doc_

financials/2024/ar/2024-Morningstar-Annual-Report.pdf/.

16 State Street Global Advisors, SPDR S&P 500 ETF Trust (SPY) Fact Sheet (2024), accessed November 6, 2025, https://www.ssga.com/library-content/products/factsheets/etfs/us/factsheet-us-en-spy.pdf.

17 Vanguard, Total Stock Market ETF (VTI) Prospectus (2024), accessed November 6, 2025, https://fund-docs.vanguard.com/F0970.pdf.

18 Vanguard Group, Vanguard Federal Money Market Fund (VMFXX) (Valley Forge, PA: Vanguard, 2024), accessed October 15, 2025, https://investor.vanguard.com/investment-products/mutual-funds/profile/vmfxx.

19 Ramsey Solutions, The National Study of Millionaires, accessed December 22, 2025, https://www.ramseysolutions.com/retirement/the-national-study-of-millionaires-research

20 Statista, Robo-Advisors—Worldwide (Hamburg: Statista GmbH, 2024), accessed October 15, 2025, https://www.statista.com/outlook/fmo/wealth-management/digital-investment/robo-advisors/worldwide

Chapter 6: Dollar Defense

21 Debt.org, "Can You File Bankruptcy on Medical Bills?," accessed October 10, 2023, https://www.debt.org/bankruptcy/medical/

ABOUT THE AUTHORS

Aaron Ross

Aaron Ross is a global keynote speaker, advisor, and bestselling author of *Predictable Revenue*—often called the "Sales Bible of Silicon Valley"—and *From Impossible to Inevitable* (co-authored with Jason Lemkin), which was named the #1 SaaS book by BookAuthority.

Aaron's sales systems have helped companies like Salesforce, Twilio, and Zuora generate billions in revenue by building scalable and predictable sales engines.

He is married with ten children—half through adoption—and lives in Edinburgh, United Kingdom.

Contact:
air@aaron-ross.co
www.linkedin.com/in/aaronross
www.fromimpossible.com/talk

Camila Farani

Camila Farani is one of Brazil's most dynamic entrepreneurs and investors, known for reshaping the country's business landscape at the intersection of technology, venture capital, and education.

A household name from her role as an investor on *Shark Tank Brasil*, Camila has invested in more than 45 companies over the past 13 years, many through her partnership at G2 Capital.

Her mission extends beyond investing. Through ventures such as Ela Vence Academy and Farani Business School, she is empowering a new generation of entrepreneurs—especially women—across Brazil.

Camila lives in Rio de Janeiro, where she balances her role as a mother with her mission to inspire and equip 40 million small business owners throughout Brazil.

Connect:
www.instagram.com/camilafarani
www.linkedin.com/in/camilafarani

Matt A. Smith

Matt A. Smith is a digital sales and marketing strategist whose career began with a startup backed by Facebook's fbFund that was later acquired.

He went on to become the first sales hire at AppSumo while earning his MBA from the Thunderbird School of Global Management.

As Senior Vice President of Sales at StackCommerce, Matt helped scale the company into a global e-commerce powerhouse—growing from a small catalog to more than 50,000 products and over $70M in annual gross merchandise value (GMV). StackCommerce was later acquired by TPG, one of the world's leading private equity firms.

Today, Matt runs Full Stack Sales, a consulting firm that helps companies scale through digital marketing, lead generation, and modern sales technology.

He lives in Coronado, California, with his wife Samantha and their puppy, Cashew.

Contact:
matt@predictableincome.io
predictableincome.io
www.linkedin.com/in/mattsmitty

Made in the USA
Monee, IL
04 November 2026

67385491R00075